Take It From the Top

What To Do With a Peak Experience

Edward M. O'Keefe Ph.D.

ISBN-10:0615665586
ISBN-13:9780615665580

DEDICATION

This book is dedicated to the memory of one of my teachers, cosmologist and eco-theologian Father Thomas Berry, C.P. (1914-2009).

Dr. Tom Berry was a scholar of Eastern religions, a cultural and religious historian, a brilliant teacher and author. His work continues to inspire and influence yet another generation of leaders and scholars in a new vision of spiritual ecology.

A peak experience when Thomas was eleven years old became the primary reference point for the rest of his life, a life of scholarly leadership and passionate concern for the salvation and nurturing of our planet.

"The universe is a communion of subjects, not a collection of objects."
>   -Thomas Berry

TABLE OF CONTENTS

INTRODUCTION

Have you ever had a peak experience, a moment of intense joy and understanding that took your breath away?

It is the thesis of this book that peak experiences or "mountain top experiences" are becoming more prevalent with each passing day, that they are happening to more and more of us, and that there are easy steps we can take to encourage and nurture more and 'bigger' ones.

I believe that peak experiences (PEs for short) are among the best and most meaningful events in our lives and that the nurturing of them is a very important means to our individual success and happiness and, at the same time, to our race's evolution and future development.

Much of what is brightest and best in our world is the direct or, at least, the indirect result of such mountain-top experiences. We will give examples in the following pages. It would not be an exaggeration to declare that PEs have been at least partly responsible for most of mankind's progress in every important area: social, economic, political, scientific, religious and spiritual.

This book presents representative examples of peak experiences from past and present, compiled from some of the well-known and some of the unknown persons to whom they've occurred and are regularly occurring. From the quite ample literature of and about PEs, we will present information about their nature and effects and about the conditions that are often – but not always – present when they occur.

The purpose of this book is to encourage you

— to jog your memory of the past.

— to dig up the backyards of the places where you grew up. (That's a metaphor or 'night language'; more about that later.)

— to remember events, especially inner events that, at least momentarily, took your breath away and made you feel wonderfully happy.

— to mine those memories (Another example of metaphorical 'night language') for gems of insight, peace and joy.

— to be open to, and more aware of further 'outbreaks of spirit' as they occur.

— to better appreciate what psychologist Abraham Maslow called "the farther reaches of human nature".

I first came upon the idea of peak experiences in the 1950s. I was teaching junior high school English at the time and had noted with great interest and alarm that statistics indicated that the prevalence of suicide among children was growing at a disturbing rate. I remembered that Abraham Maslow, who had coined the phrase 'peak experience', had made this statement: "The peak experience (is) so high that it justifies living itself. Peak experiences can make life worthwhile by their occasional occurrence. They give meaning to life itself. They prove it is worthwhile. *To say this in a negative way, I would guess that peak experiences help to prevent suicide.*" (Italics added)

From that point on, I became enamored by these mountain-top moments. I studied the research; I began collecting examples of them, both in literature and in 'real life'; I assigned students, both in junior high school and later in the college where I taught, to write about theirs. When students shared their experiences with their peers, classroom magic happened! Vitality and life erupted! It was clear that students were immensely 'turned on' by thinking about and recounting these special experiences. Discussion was never so rich nor so meaningful.

So began a lifelong passion which culminates in this book.

The purpose of this book is to encourage you, the readers to become more aware of mountain-top experiences, to look for, think about, and appreciate transpersonal states that have affected you and your fellow humans.

Such an activity will change and enhance your concepts of what it means to be human, which will not only positively affect your own self-image, but also will enable you to become better attuned to the great potential of every person and the entire human race. You will be stimulated and inspired as you read the descriptions of the peak experiences that have so greatly transformed the lives of those whom you will read about.

One of the contributors to this work, Suka Chapel, whose account of one of her peak experiences will be found in Chapter 9, "Wired For the Transcendent", wrote this to the author, concisely illustrating one of our purposes in producing this book:

Thank you for encouraging me to write about this. It occurred 26 years ago and I've never written about it. As you said it would, the memory and the writing brought so much joy and hope back to my heart. One never forgets such an experience. I believe it is a gift we are given to remind us of whence we came and where we are destined to return and to keep plodding along, no matter how slowly, toward that promised life that is our only true reality.

As the college students in Professor Abraham Maslow's classes at Brandeis University remembered and related the PEs they had experienced in their earlier lives, more memories of them came to mind, and, also, fresh ones were experienced. It is my hope - and really my knowing – the same will happen to you. As the ancient adage puts it, "What You Think About, Grows."

I wish you a pleasant journey through this book and through the memories of your own mountain-top experiences.

PLAN OF THE BOOK

After defining and describing peak experiences (PEs) in chapter 1, we shall consider the language difficulties of speaking and writing about these episodes often described as ineffable (chapter 2).

Chapters 3 to 6 will provide a potpourri of many varieties of PEs described by well-known, little known or unknown persons. These mountain-top moments were occasioned by the beauties of nature, music, sports, death and sorrow, birth and elation – the whole list of human events that we all experience. Many happen to children, covered in chapter 5.

Chapter 7 will highlight some of reasons why we don't experience more PEs, and what we can do to counter these barriers to the growth of the human spirit. Then we will list five steps we might take to increase their number and power in our lives (8).

In chapter 9 we will consider how PEs relate to transcendence, to spirituality, to mystical states of consciousness and to what Abraham Maslow called "the higher reaches of human nature".

We will outline four possible theories (chapter 10) to explain how these strange and significant events happen. The final chapter (11) will consider the role of PEs in the evolutionary march of the human spirit.

Chapter One

WHAT ARE PEAK EXPERIENCES?

We begin with three examples of PEs from the life of environmentalist "Amazon John" Easterling. He is the founder of the Amazon Herb Company and now leads a group of eco-entrepreneurs in efforts to save the Amazon rainforest. He also supports ten indigenous communities in securing deeds and titles to their land by supplying funds for surveying and for legal costs. He is married to entertainer Olivia Newton-John, also a devoted environmentalist.

He attributes his passion for the environment of the Amazon River in Brazil and his recovery from major health challenges to three major peak experiences that have guided him through his life.

The <u>first</u> occurred in third grade when his class read in the current Weekly Reader about Sangrog, a South American boy who cared for his llamas in the snowcapped Andes Mountains. The story fascinated young John and his mind raced with the possibilities. In his heart he knew he had found his passion and destiny …in South America.

1

(As we shall see, many life-changing peak experiences - PEs - occur to the young. Note also the phrase "in his heart he *knew*"; PEs usually involve a deep knowing.)

After graduating from the University of North Carolina with a degree in environmental science, he took the first of over 180 trips to South America (as of May 2009). He crisscrossed the Andes for years searching for lost cities and Pre-Columbian civilizations.

The <u>second</u> major altered state event occurred when Easterling was apparently dying from the potentially fatal Rocky Mountain spotted fever.

...Easterling suddenly found himself in darkness, flying across the surface of a slick lake towards a moon in the distance. Zooming towards the light, *he realized he was in the presence of God. Easterling experienced an expansion of his awareness that brought him answers to his burning questions about the ancient Incan and Mayan civilizations.* As he basked in the Presence, he understood that love and forgiveness were most important. He also realized it was not his time to leave the human world... Easterling said of that experience that he is no longer afraid of dying and, perhaps more importantly, he is no longer afraid of all-out living.

(Note that this might also be classified as a near death experience – NDE – and/or an out-of-body experience – OOBE. Many 'peakers' report losing any fear of dying after their PEs.)

On a third occasion, while traveling deep inside the Amazon rainforest, "Amazon John", still not in good health, was struck down by fever and was nursed back to health in an indigenous native village. The powerful medicine of healing teas made from the rainforest plants made him whole again. He continued his travel further upriver.

As he stepped out of his dugout canoe into the jungle, a profound realization overtook him: the treasure he sought was in the plants of the rainforest he'd been cutting down with his machete while looking for lost civilizations. In that moment, his entire life changed once again....

Amazon John is a man on a mission, guided by a powerful vision: to preserve one million acres of rainforest and to empower the indigenous people to make their own choices about their children's future and the land of their ancestors. (Italics added)

- Jennifer Hadley, "Man On a Mission"
from Science of Mind,
December 2008. pp.94-98

The term "peak experience" was coined by American psychologist Abraham Maslow (1908 – 1970). He is well known for his conceptualization of a "hierarchy of human needs" and is considered the founder of Humanistic Psychology.

While in his late thirties, Maslow was struck by the thought that modern psychology was based on the study of sick people - neurotics, psychotics and generally unhappy people with emotional or mental problems. Since most people are not sick, he mused, wouldn't it be of value to study and analyze healthy people with healthy minds?

In a letter to British author Colin Wilson, Maslow stated,

When I started to explore the psychology of health, I picked out the finest, healthiest people, the best specimens of mankind I could find and studied them to see what they were like. They were very different, in some ways startlingly different from the average...

I learned many lessons from these people. But one in particular is our concern now. I found that these individuals tended to report having had something like mystical experiences, moments of great awe, moments of the most intense happiness, or even rapture, ecstasy or bliss...

These moments were of pure, positive happiness, when all doubts, all fears, all inhibitions, all tensions, all weaknesses, were left behind. Now self-consciousness was lost. All separateness and distance for the world disappeared as they felt one with the world, fused with it, really belonging to it, instead of being outside, looking in... Perhaps the most important of all, however, was the report in these experiences of the feeling that they had really seen the ultimate truth, the essence of things, the secret of life, as if veils had been pulled aside. (Wilson, New Pathways in Psychology, pp. 8,9)

Maslow studied these "healthiest" people, whom he termed "self-actualized", for many years and continued to note their many peak experiences. In later life he came to believe that many people of lesser achievement also had peak experiences, that PEs were more common that he had originally thought.

Here are three brief PE's reported by Maslow.

1. A young mother is scurrying around her kitchen and getting breakfast for her husband and young children. The sun was streaming in; the children, neat and nicely dressed, were chattering as they ate. The husband was casually playing with the children. As she looked at them she was suddenly so overwhelmed with their beauty and her great love for them, and her feeling of good fortune, that she went into a peak experience...

2. A young man working his way through medical school by drumming in a jazz band reported many years later that in

all his drumming he had three peaks when he suddenly felt like a great drummer and his performance was perfect.

3. A hostess after a dinner party where everything had gone perfectly and it had been a fine evening, said goodbye to her last guest, sat down in a chair, looked around at the mess, and went into a peak of great happiness and exhilaration. (Wilson, New Pathways, p. 17)

Peak experiences are difficult to define or precisely describe. They are extraordinary (i.e. out of the ordinary) positive experiences reported by large numbers of human beings. By common agreement of all PE researchers since Richard Bucke and William James, these mountain-top experiences refer only to *positive* "out of the ordinary" experiences. So we are not referring to nightmares, negative visions, scary apparitions, etc. PEs, though they might upset and startle us for a while, result in happiness and joy. They are most often of short duration – seconds, minutes, sometimes days, rarely more than a few days. Having tasted the sweetness of such extraordinary events, 'peakers' uniformly express great disappointment and sorrow when they fade.

Author C.S. Lewis in Surprised By Joy, writes eloquently of the fleetingness of PEs, and, above all, of the pure joy that is felt and the tremendous frustration and longing to reawaken the joy of the experience. But PEs are, almost by definition, non-repeatable. A later chapter will consider the extent to which they can be solicited and actively sought after.

Examples from Abraham Maslow's Mountain-Top Moments

Once, in a speech made late in his life, Maslow uncharacteristically spoke of three of his own peak experiences: 1.) "...his poignant awareness of the evanescence of individual existence before eternity as he had stood watching the ocean waves and surf several weeks

before. He found himself quivering as he talked. (2) When he began to speak of his thoughts about his infant grand-daughter, he became so emotional that it was hard for him to continue. (3) He spoke too of a transcendent vision he had experienced at a Brandeis graduation ceremony some years back: in the distance of his mind's eye, he saw a long procession of scholars and thinkers – going all the way back to Socrates, Plato, and Aristotle and stretching far, far into the future of yet unborn generations – and he had felt a serene joy in seeing himself a part of this unbroken line."
(Hoffman, <u>The Right to be Human</u>, p.331)

The word "ecstasy" is often used to describe mountain-top moments. Spiritual writer Matthew Fox equates PEs with ecstasy, a word that connotes other-worldly connection.

...an ecstatic experience is one of forgetting oneself and of being turned on in a full and deep way. Our ecstasy is our getting outside ourselves (the word comes from two Greek words meaning 'to stand outside of'), our forgetting ourselves – if only for a second, a minute, an hour, a day... or a lifetime. Ecstasy is our getting high. For this very reason, because ecstasy is a forgetting, it is also memorable. Ecstasy is a memorable experience of forgetting oneself, of getting outside of oneself. Our ecstatic experiences, then, are the memorable experiences of our lives. (Fox, <u>Wee, we, Whee All the Way Home</u>, p. 43, 44)

Because mountain-top experiences are so difficult to adequately define, we present below some of the terms and phrases used to describe them.

Terms/Phrases Used to Describe Peak Experiences

A birth into a new and wider world, full of unsuspected possibilities - Pierro Ferrucci
A bubbling over of sheer delight – Abraham Maslow
A moment of timeless awareness of our true nature – Romella Hart
A temporary period of extreme mental health – Abraham Maslow
An illumination that dispels all illusion – Pierro Ferrucci
A radiant riot of the all-encompassing – Ken Wilbur
A sort of ecstasy – Leonard Bernstein
A sudden surge of meaning – Colin Wilson, British author
Absurd good news - G.K. Chesterton
A visitation of God – Robert A, Johnson
Astral projection
Being one with a Ground of Being, one with spirit, one with infinity – Ken Wilbur
Confrontation with the eternal – Irina Starr
Contact with the transpersonal
Cosmic consciousness – Richard Bucke
Ecstasy – Andrew Greeley
Enlightenment
Experiences of the numinous – Rudolf Otto
Extraordinarily lucid moments of grace
Footprints of God – Barbara Bradley Haggerty
Healing bliss
Moments of radical amazement – Abraham Heschel, Jewish theologian
Moments of pure, positive happiness when all doubts, all fears, all inhibitions, all weaknesses are left behind – Abraham Maslow
Near-death Experiences (NDEs)
Outbreaks of joy
Outbreaks of spirit

> Out of body experiences (OOBEs)
> Slivers of eternity – Ardis Whitman
> Surprised by joy – C.S. Lewis
> Transcendental experiences – Irina Starr
> Transformation
> When we feel one with the heart of the universe – Ardis Whitman

THE FARTHER REACHES OF HUMAN NATURE

Ken Wilbur, American philosopher and founder of the Integral Institute, makes helpful distinctions to assist our understanding of peak experiences. In his Introduction to <u>The Translucent Revolution</u> by Arjuna Ardagh (2005), Wilber says that we learned at least three lessons from the human potential movement of the last thirty years. They are summarized here:

1. STATES OF CONSCIOUSNESS

There are many different states of consciousness: ordinary (awake, sleeping, dreaming, etc.) and "altered", i.e. stoned, meditative, contemplative, hypnogogic, entrained, "flow", awakened states, transformative states culminating in Enlightenment (non-dual/ Unity) states.

> **Serious writers and researchers henceforth could never pretend that there was simply one world lying around waiting to be perceived. ...(T)he world that is perceived is a co-creation of your consciousness. Change your consciousness and you change your world. (p. xiv)**

2. STAGES OF CONSCIOUSNESS

In addition to passing, shifting <u>states</u> of consciousness, there are more stable graduated <u>stages</u> of consciousness available to humans. "Stages are the way that evolution catapults over chaos and into increasing spheres of organization and inclusion". Each stage includes the already earned progress of its predecessor.

Wilbur calls some of these stages in human development: egocentric, ethnocentric, worldcentric, and kosmocentric.

In the past, Wilbur continues:

We just didn't know the embrace could go all the way to infinity. But that is exactly what the human potential movement discovered: in the farther reaches of human nature, in the realms of the self-transcendence needs, in the deepest reaches of your very own Self and your ever-present I AM-ness, people reported being one with a Ground of Being, one with Spirit, one with infinity, a radiant riot of the all-encompassing, call it what you will. (p. xvii)

3. ALTERED STATES OFTEN OCCUR RANDOMLY

Although the states and stage of consciousness may seem hierarchical in nature, altered states are sometimes more random that one might expect.

...Researchers soon found that virtually anybody can have those peak awakening experiences, even people at the ethnocentric stages, and all it did was make them more ethnocentric....*You can have a profound altered state experience at virtually any stage you are at...*

For example, if you are at an ethnocentric stage of development and you have a unity-state experience of being one with everything or one with a ground of being, you might interpret that as an experience of oneness with Jesus and conclude that nobody can be saved unless they accept Jesus as their personal savior (hence the "ethnocentric" nature of the

9

> interpretation – you must belong to this one group in order to be saved). But if you are in an egocentric stage and have the same experience, you might believe that you yourself *are* Jesus Christ. And if you are at a kosmocentric or integral stage and have that nondual peak experience, you will likely conclude that you and all sentient beings without exception are one with spirit in the timeless here and now. (p xvii)

We are reminded of Aristotle's dictum that everything is received according to the manner of the one receiving it.

While acknowledging that peak experiences may have the effect of reinforcing the narrowness of whatever state of consciousness the 'peaker' may be at, Wilbur joins other students/scholars of PEs to extol the value and personal worth of experiencing awakened states.

> ...(R)esearch also found a riveting fact: the more you are dunked into altered or nonordinary or meditative states, the more quickly you actually move through any stage sequence that was tested,...the more translucent you will become.

Ken Wilbur concludes his remarks with this advice:

> If you choose to grow at all, you must begin to open yourself to wider experiences, deeper truths, higher realizations; and allow yourself – or push yourself, or simply nudge yourself – into wider states of consciousness and attitudes and perspectives and experiences. (p xviii)

We will return to this important subject in later chapters.

PEAK EXPERIENCES AND RELIGION

Are peak experiences not God speaking to us? What else can account for such extraordinary events in our lives?

Are PE's mystical states of consciousness, breakthrough messages from God? Are they not intimately connected to spiritual progress? Are not blissful experiences of the unity of all things essentially "God experiences"? Are they not examples of what author Barbara Bradley Haggerty calls "Footsteps of God"? Isn't Wordsworth correct to speak of them as "intimations of Immortality"?

On the pro-religionist side of the argument is a centuries-old rich tradition of Eastern and Western mysticism attested to by numberless and profound saints and scholars. In this view, mystical, often miraculous, mountain-top experiences are seen as markers along the path to transformation into God, whether the path is completed in one or multiple lives. Most of the listings in this book's bibliography relate PEs to religion, transcendence and mystical union with God. However, the Eastern tradition is largely omitted from this book; unfortunately, even a review of this voluminous literature goes far beyond our scope.

It is also clear that most, if not all, religions begin and initially develop with the profound peak experiences of their founders and/or early adherents. One example from the Old Testament is the story of Moses being given the Ten Commandments during a purportedly actual mountain-top experience. Compare in the New Testament the story of Jesus' transfiguration: "As (Jesus) was praying, the appearance of his face changed, and his clothes became as bright as a flash of lightning". (Luke 9:28-36) Also, "miracles" and large numbers of healings were brought about by Jesus and his early followers, according to the New Testament authors.

Many of the examples of mountain top experiences in this book were perceived by the 'peakers' as profoundly moving religious events that most often changed completely their lives, perceptions and understandings. However, the person most responsible for the study of PEs, Abraham Maslow, was an articulate and committed atheist and saw things differently. Many scientists, researchers and others who study PE's, whether theistic, non-theistic or agnostic themselves, also do not believe that supernatural interventions are required to account for even the most exalted mystical experiences.

> Miracles are not an intervention in the divine order, but a calling into play of laws beyond our present understanding. It has been said that the miracles of today are the science of tomorrow. An automobile, a television, even the lighting of a match would have been a miracle to those of Jesus's time.
>
> Peter Calhoun, <u>Soul on Fire</u>, p. 7

Scientist Charles T. Tart has spent more than 50 years studying the paranormal. In his introduction to <u>Journeys Out of the Body</u> by Robert Monroe, Tart speaks of the natural tendency of those we have called 'peakers' to relate their experiences, not of what actually happened to them, but of what they thought it meant. Since many PEs are not only profound but loaded with religious import, the experiencer uses the language of his particular religious background.

As an example, let us suppose that what really happens to a person is that he finds himself floating in the air above his body, in the middle of the night; while still surprised at this, he perceives a shadowy, dim figure at the end of the room, and then a blue circle of light floats past the figure from left to right. Then our experiencer loses consciousness and wakes up in his body. A good reporter will describe essentially that scene. Many people will say, in perfectly good faith, something like, 'My immortal soul was raised from the tomb of my body by the grace of God last night, and an angel appeared. As a symbol of God's favor, the angel showed me a symbol of wholeness.'

I have often seen distortions this great when I've been able to question an individual about what exactly happened, but most of the published accounts of out-of-body-experiences (OOBEs) have not been subject to this kind of questioning. The statements that God's will caused the OOBE , that the

dim figure turned into an angel, that the blue circle was a symbol of wholeness, are all part of a person's *interpretation,* not his *experience.* Most people are not aware of the extent to which their mind automatically interprets things. They think they are perceiving things as they are. (from Tart's Introduction to Journeys Out of the Body by Robert Monroe, PP. 6,7)

> Stories communicate at seven different levels of meaning depending on the level of spiritual development of the listener.
> - Sufi Belief

However, priest, sociologist, and researcher Andrew Greeley has this to say about those peak experiences that seem to have a mystic, otherworld quality to them:

The mystical experience seems to be reasonably common. It involves a breaking away from daily experience of time and place and a search for some sort of basic and primitive union with the Way Things Really Are. *While in its origins it was certainly religious, it need not be religious for people today, in the sense that it need not have a special theological or denominational context.*

However, in its attempt to come to grips experientially with the Way Things Really Are, the mystical interlude is implicitly and fundamentally religious....It is usually triggered by some sort of experience of goodness, truth, beauty, or pleasure that apparently predisposes the person for the mystical event by taking his mind off ordinary events and making him temporarily passive so that "reality may rush in." When that rushing in occurs, the person has the sense of being seized by ... something that takes control of the whole personality. Peace, joy, union, insight, love, confidence seem to take possession of the person. If the context of the experience is Christian, there also seems to come a reassurance of personal survival; if the context is Eastern, the dominant impression may be one of union, of being merged with a great cosmic reality. Finally the ecstatic 'comes down' for his moments of rapture with new serenity and confidence for this everyday life. (Italics added.) (Greeley, Ecstasy: A Way of Knowing p.47, 48)

We will have much more to say throughout this book about the relationship between our understanding of peak experiences and the realm of religion and religious beliefs. Before going on, however, it is necessary to speak of one kind of peak experience that is growing in numbers literally every day as a result of scientific developments in the field of medicine and medical care.

PEAK EXPERIENCES NEAR DEATH – NDEs

Nearly 30 years ago, Pollster George Gallop, Jr. discovered that nearly 5% of the adult population in North America have had a near-death experience (NDE). (N-Gallop, Adventures in Immortality, 1982) Thus there are literally hundreds of thousands of people alive today who have experienced NDEs which, though sometimes varying in detail, have so many common elements to reported PEs that we consider them a form of peak experience. Researchers estimate that about one-third of the adults who face death, nearly die, or who are later resuscitated have a near-death experience.

The near-death experience is an awareness, sense, or experience of 'otherworldliness', ... that happens to people who are at the edge of death. It is of such magnitude that most experiencers are deeply affected – many to the point of making significant changes in their lives afterwards because of what they went through. (Atwater, The Complete Idiot's Guide to Near-Death Experiences, p. 7)

According to Raymond Moody, author of the landmark book, <u>Life After Life</u> (1975), there are most often 15 common elements reported by near-death experiencers. Moody, by the way, coined the term 'near-death experience'.

- Ineffability, beyond the limits of any language to describe.
- Hearing yourself pronounced dead
- Feelings of peace and quiet
- Hearing unusual noises
- Seeing a dark tunnel
- Finding your self outside your body
- Meeting "spiritual beings"
- A very bright light experienced as a "being of light"
- A panoramic life review
- Sensing a border or limit to where you can go
- Coming back into your body
- Frustrating attempts to tell others about what happened to you
- Subtle broadening and deepening of your life afterward
- Elimination of the fear of death
- Corroboration of events witnessed while out of your body

Near-death experiences, since they are happening much more often because modern medical techniques are allowing people to "return" from the realm of the dying, are assisting us to become more familiar with at least some of the 'natural' forms of altered states of consciousness.

> The study of transpersonal states changes our concept of what it means to be human, and therefore changes our image of ourselves and other people. ...We realize that these experiences do not strictly belong to individuals far removed from us in space and time but that, at least potentially, they reside in us as well. — Pierro Ferrucci, Inevitable Grace p. 11)

Paul Pearson, in his book, <u>Wishing Well</u> , speaks of "near-life experiences, tantalizing brushes with some sense of the supernatural that breaks through our high sixth-sense threshold. It's usually something about nature's magnificent beauty and power that causes these NLEs; perhaps a gorgeous sunset, an arching rainbow, a shooting star, the birth of a child, or the passing of a loved one." (p.67)

SUMMARY OF CHAPTER ONE   *We have briefly attempted to define and describe what Abraham Maslow termed 'peak experience', a concept difficult to fully explain in our normal language categories. Philosopher Ken Wilbur has helped elucidate the phrase by analyzing the concept in terms of the states and stages of consciousness available to human beings. The interface between PEs and religious experiences was touched upon. (Much more will be said about this matter throughout the book.) Finally, we pointed out that the number of reported transcendental experiences have been dramatically increasing, partly because many more near-death experiences (NDEs) are being reported due to the successes of modern medical procedures that are able to intervene with the death process as we have understood it, and resuscitate people who would otherwise have died. We will suggest later that there may well be other reasons behind the rapid increase in reported PEs.*

In the next chapter we will deal with the difficulties of adequately describing peak experiences in human language.

Chapter Two

DAY AND NIGHT

THE LANGUAGES OF REASON AND REVERENCE

> ineffable: Adj.   1. That which cannot be expressed in speech.
> 2. That which must not be spoken; too lofty or sacred for
> expression. (Webster's Dictionary)

The phenomena of peak experiences, which exist in every clime and culture, immediately raise significant problems concerning the inadequacy of human language. PEs, by their very nature, are difficult, sometimes impossible, to fully express in language. Frustrated by the limitations of left hemisphere literalism, only the metaphorical language of poetry seems in any way adequate to express the richness and nuances of mountain-top experiences.

Adding to the difficulty of conveying deep and profound experiences are the limitations on understanding that arise from the language and cultural constructs which we all harbor. Centuries ago, the philosopher Aristotle posited as a maxim that "Everything is received after the manner of the one receiving it". To say this in more modern terminology, we humans interpret everything that happens to us according to what we already know or think we know. So our personal experiences, our cultural and family values, our educational and social backgrounds – all these, and much more - highly influence the way we understand and interpret our reality, including, of course, our peak experiences.

An example of this occurs in Abraham Maslow's letter, already quoted, to Colin Wilson. As Maslow became aware of the prevalence of PEs among his self-actualized subjects, he acknowledged his earlier biased pre-conceptions, unfortunately still rampant in many scientists like himself:

> **...The little that I ever read about mystical experiences tied them with religion, with visions of the supernatural. And, like most scientists, I had sniffed at them in disbelief and considered it all nonsense, maybe hallucinations, maybe hysteria – almost certainly pathological.**

> **But the people telling me...about these experiences were not such people – they were the healthiest people! And I may add that it taught me something about the limitations of the small...orthodox scientist who won't recognize as knowledge, or as reality, any information that doesn't fit into the already existent science. (2-1)**

A third major communication problem with conveying peak experiences is the obvious tie-in with religion and spirituality. PEs are very often, perhaps most often, received, perceived and understood as profoundly moving mystical experiences from other than this world's sources, requiring the use of extraordinary superlatives, almost a meta-language, to express and discuss. Some religionists, for example, believe that any personal or communal guidance received via peaks, comes directly from the Most High God. Most scholars of the phenomena, however, even priests such as sociologist Father Andrew Greeley, see no need or evidence that even a belief in a divine being is necessary for their occurrence. It is ironic that, because religious beliefs are immediately involved, PEs, even though so often linked with a profoundly felt knowledge of our unity with one another and with the universe, can themselves be a source of misunderstanding, division and separation.

To begin with the linguistic problem, we note a helpful approach supplied by Michael Dowd in his deservedly celebrated 2007 book, Thank God For Evolution. Dowd uses the terms 'Day Language' and 'Night Language' to distinguish

> ...the complementary sides of the one coin of our experience. On one side is the realm of what's so: the facts, the objectively real, that which is publicly and measurable true. Let's call this side of our reality our *day experience.* We talk and write about it using *day language* – that is, normal everyday discourse. The other side of our experiential coin I call *night experience.* It is communicated through *night language*, by way of grand metaphors, poetry, and vibrant images. Our attention is focused on 'What does it mean?' This side of our experience is subjectively real, like a nighttime dream, though not objectively real. Night language is personally or culturally meaningful. It nourishes us with spectacular images of emotional truth.
>
> ...Whenever we think or talk about an event, there is always A) what happened, B) the story about what happened and C) the meaning we make out of the story of what happened.
>
> (pp.113,114)

Dowd calls day and night language, respectively, the language of reason and the language of reverence. He further distinguishes between private and public revelation. "Private revelation is grounded in subjective experience and is expressed in traditional, religious, night language. Public revelation is grounded in objective experience; it is measurable and verifiable and is expressed in day language" (p.114). If we can make this distinction, people's descriptions of peak experiences are not as likely to jar our religious and cultural sensitivities.

> "I can hear the sizzle of a new-born star and know that anything of meaning, of fierce magic, is emerging here. I am witness to flexible eternity, the evolving past, and I know I will live forever – as dust or breath in the face of stars, in the shifting patterns of wind."
>
> -Poet Jo Harjo, using night language

Writer e e cummings did not want his poetry to have the normal capitalization, punctuation and diction because he wanted to jolt his readers into a different-than-normal state of consciousness so they could be receptive to his night language. An example of cumming's unusual use of language (and probably the expression of one of his own profound mountaintop experiences) follows.

> i thank You God for most this amazing
> day: for the leaping greenly spirits of trees
> And a blue true dream of sky; and for everything
> which is natural which is infinite which is you

As in reading poetry, the reader of a collection of PEs is invited to enter a state of consciousness that is open to metaphorical language, to night language, to more or less faltering attempts to ground the grandiose, to pronounce the profound, to express the ineffable. Perhaps Samuel Taylor Coleridge's advice for enjoying literature is even more appropriate here – maintain "a willing suspension of disbelief" – so that other levels of consciousness, deeper layers of transcendent reality, may engulf your heart as well as your mind.

———

MADDENING ADJECTIVE – "INDESCRIBABLE"

In her 2006 best seller, <u>Eat, Pray, Love</u>, author Elizabeth Gilbert speaks of her frustration in reading others' attempts to describe "that moment in which the soul excuses itself from time and place and merges with the infinite....Often you see the maddening adjective, 'indescribable' used to describe the event." (p.189)

She then goes on to describe, in picturesque night language, one of her own transformative peak experiences. She adroitly uses such wonderfully descriptive phrases as:

> ...I got pulled through the wormhole of the Absolute...

> ...I was inside the void, but I was also the void and I was looking at the void, all at the same time. The void was a place of limitless peace and wisdom. The void was conscious and it was intelligent. The void was God, which means that I was inside God. I was both a tiny piece of the universe and exactly the same size as the universe. ...

She concludes,

> I wondered, "Why have I been chasing happiness my whole life when bliss was right here the entire time?'
> (pp.199, 200)

———

Many writers describing mountain-top moments use poetry, the language of metaphor, in an attempt to convey the ineffable in words. Consider this attempt, by an anonymous contributor, to express divine visitations. He uses night language and repetition effectively.

Nocturnal Visits

Sometimes in the late hours
When the world is mostly slumbering
Your love comes over me like pure white doves
With sweetness that touches the very core of me.

I am transfixed by your beauty
The joy of your gentle touch
The depths of your loving kindness
The softness of your glistening stardew.

If this love were color it would be rainbow
If texture, the smoothness of infant skin
If this love were music it would be rhapsody
Played on angel harps of gold.

But words fail to convey its essence
Thought cannot follow this love's flow
I am enveloped by its total majesty
Overwhelmed by the onrush of joy.

Sometimes in the late hours
When the world is mostly slumbering
You visit me with floods of solace and
I am filled with the quality of Thee.

———————

As we sample this collection of PEs, alert readers will perceive the peakers' struggle with language as they try to put words around ideas and feelings from the outer edges of our perceived reality, from, in Maslow's phrase, "the farther reaches of human nature." Only night language will suffice, and, often no human language will be adequate.

———————

Here is another example. The author of the next piece uses verse to express what she described as a powerful transpersonal event experienced when she swam with two dolphins in November, 1991. The gifts she refers to in the first stanza were a lump of coral and a mangrove pod.

Delphi and Kibby

The sun sets over the Gulf
highlighting the puffy clouds along the horizon.
The dolphins come to me with their gifts
and we make dolphin-love.

They dive under my hand
descending ever so slowly
so that my hand guides over every inch of their backs
and caresses their flukes.

Then he surfaces in greeting.
As my hand touches his head.
His eyes close
and the rub begins.

He's close as I gently massage his head
And my hand gets close to his pectoral.
He ever so slowly
rolls over.

Not once does he open his eyes
as I caress the tender skin of his throat and chest.
His fins shudder as I tickle him
And I hear him smiling.

Over and over he rolls
in sublime slow motion.
All time may stop and the world be still
in this experience of total trust and connectedness.

As darkness descends I must leave them
but I take their spirits and their lessons into my world.
The most subtle messages are the most powerful…
Love, Joy, Trust, Spirit, and the connectedness of all things.

Bobbi Abbott

INEFFABILITY – AN HISTORICAL EXAMPLE

Perhaps some of the most profound peak experiences have not been reported because of the inability of human language to express some of 'the farther reaches of human nature'. Consider, for example, the case of St. Thomas Aquinas, the most famous and best known Catholic theologian and scholar of all time. He was a Dominican priest who lived in the 13th Century (1225-1274). His 'magnum opus' was the <u>Summa Theologica</u>, considered even today the definitive exposition of Catholic doctrine which is still being taught in every Catholic seminary in the world.

On December 6, 1273, the year before he died at age 49, Thomas had a vision while saying Mass in Naples, Italy. He reported that Jesus appeared to him. After that transcendent moment, which he was unable to describe any further, Thomas stopped writing and lecturing. He told his colleague and scribe that he was unable to write another word, "because all that I have written in the past seems to me now like so much straw."

———

> "What it comes down to is that what is experienced is what is known. In the experience itself, there is no doubt. In talking about the experience, on the other hand, the mind needs much assistance from the heart to point to the reality that was so obvious...The poet and the artist have as much, if not more, authority than the philosopher or the theologian in such matters.
> James Nourse, Simple Spirituality, pp.125,126

SUMMARY OF CHAPTER TWO *How can we humans speak of eternity, of the transpersonal, of angels and God without using 'night language', metaphorical language, the language of awe and reverence? It must be so. Otherwise, if God can fit into our left brain categories, is not our God too small? Otherwise, would we not be like horses discussing among themselves what humans are like, how they think, what they do?*

'Peakers', as we will see, cannot be limited to everyday language, left-brain, totally literal words and meanings, and still be true to their visions, their insights, their glimpses into other realities. The distinction, borrowed from Michael Dowd, between day and night language will help us as we move forward.

Having pointed out the language difficulties, we are ready to begin the joyful testimonies of dozens of 'peakers' who share with us their moments of awe.

Chapter Three

PEs OF MUSIC AND PERFORMANCE

After religious/spiritual events and Nature itself, music stands out as the most profound trigger for transformative experiences. Hundreds, perhaps thousands, of examples dot our collective and individual human histories. All types of music seem capable of producing individual and, often, group peak experiences.

I have had a few peak experiences in my life. One came at a Bruce Springsteen concert. It really was incredible. Everybody there was dancing their heart out. We were all one and one was all. Everybody there was having the best time of their lives singing and dancing. It was like a big party

and all the people there were best friends. I recall just walking up to strangers and starting to dance. It was electric.

– Sean Brophy, Student

"Our tradition teaches us that sound is God – Nada Brahma. That is, musical sound and the musical experience are steps to the realization of the self. We view music as a kind of spiritual discipline that raises one's inner being to divine peacefulness and bliss…The highest aim of our music is to reveal the essence of the universe it reflects, and the ragas are among the means by which this essence can be apprehended. Thus, through music, one can reach God."   - Ravi Shankar

---

JULIE ANDREWS — "AS ADDICTIVE AS OPIUM"

The well known singer/actress Julie Andrews, in the passage below from her 2008 autobiography, Home: A Memoir of My Early Years eloquently provides the bridge between the effects of music on the listeners and the often even more powerful experiences on the composers who create and the artists who perform the music.

Once in a while I experience an emotion onstage that is so gut-wrenching, so heart-stopping, that I could weep with gratitude and joy. The feeling catches and magnifies so rapidly that it threatens to engulf me.

It starts as a bass note, resonating deep in my system. Literally. It's like the warmest, lowest sound from a contrabass. There is a sudden thrill of connection and an awareness of size – the theater itself, more the height of the great stage housing behind and above me, where history has been absorbed, where darkness contains mystery and light has meaning. Light is a part of it...to be flooded with it, to absorb it and allow it through the body. The dust that has a smell so thick and evocative, one feels one could almost eat it; makeup and sweat, perfume and paint; the vast animal that is an audience, warm and pulsing, felt but unseen.

Most of all, it is the music – when a great sweep of sound makes you attempt things that earlier in the day you might never have thought possible. When the orchestra swells to support your voice, when the melody is perfect and the words so right there could not possibly be any others, when a modulation occurs and lifts you to an even higher plateau...it is bliss. And that is the moment to share it.

One senses the audience feels it, too, and together you ride the ecstasy all the way home....

Then I think there is no more magical feeling, no one luckier than I. It is to do with the joy of being a vessel, being used, using oneself fully and totally in the service of something that brings wonder. If only one could experience this every night.

It is as great as sex...that moment before climax. It is as overwhelming as the mighty ocean. As nurturing as mother's milk to an infant. As addictive as opium.

(pp. 265, 266)

———

Musical performance peaks are in no way limited to professional artists like Julie Andrews. The gift is apparently given, not so much for the quality of the performance, but is offered, whenever it comes, to amateurs or to anybody involved. The following comes from a former student of the author's, in his twenties at the time.

POSSESSED BY SOME WILD SPIRITS

I reach "the peak'" only sometimes when I play music with my band. We practice often (two or three times a week) and often we don't put our hearts and souls into it. That's when it's ordinary and almost boring.

But sometimes something just clicks on. It seems like we are all possessed by some wild spirits that want to have fun and they use us as their tools. It can happen anytime we are tuning our instruments, in the middle of a performance, or while we are just warming up. Not a word is spoken; our instruments do all the talking. The music we play in those moments goes beyond our normal abilities; it's full of power and rich harmony. A song that we may have played dozens of times sounds totally different in the "crazy high" we all experience. There is also a strong feeling of union because we all feel like vital parts of a body that we created and that could not live without each one of us.

After a little while, our tired, crazy spirits go away and we look at each other, half smiling and thinking "I sounded great, we all sounded great" Then we try to bring back this "high", but it's gone until who knows when.

-Dan Pasteur

Abraham Maslow was himself a great lover of music and often sang its praises in ecstatic phrases.

Music, let it be known, is an end to itself and not a means to an end! I hear 200 voices and 100 instruments screaming to the open heavens the joy that was Beethoven. I hear Debussy reproduce for us an exquisite mood of delicious warm languor. I hear a Mozart minuet and the whole dainty, precious era is conjured up before my mind....Music, for me, is the highest of the arts. It is to me one of the reasons for living. One of the most important, even in comparison with love, the most important of all ends of life." (Hoffman, The Right To Be Human – p.21)

———————

LEONARD BERNSTEIN ——"A SORT OF ECSTASY"

Composer and conductor Leonard Bernstein described how the experience of conducting a large orchestra often affected him.

At the end of such performances, performances which I call good, it takes minutes before I know where I am – in what hall, in what country – or who I am. Suddenly I become aware that there is clapping, that I must bow. It's very difficult. But marvelous. *A sort of ecstasy which is nothing more and nothing less than a loss of ego.* You don't exist. It's exactly the same sort of ecstasy as the trance you were in when you are composing and you are inspired. You don't know what time it is or what's going on. (Italics added) (quoted in Ferrucci, Inevitable Grace, p.17)

———————

PERFORMANCE PEAKS REPORTED BY COLLEGE STUDENTS/MUSICIANS

At our first public performance, I was petrified. But when the drum started to beat, something strange happened. I lost my fear completely. We were all filled with confidence and assurance that we could do it. We finished the entire set with no mistakes. After the gig, people came up to talk to us. I stood there looking at my amp and feeling like the center of the world.

Sometimes I've had similar feelings since. But only while I'm playing. When it comes, I feel like I'm one with the music I'm playing. In fact, *I feel like I AM the music*.

- David Howard

I am in the music business. Doing shows and doing great shows have only one difference---peak experiences. Just before peaks come, I can feel them coming and I get the group to quickly get into the next song. It feels like the audience knows exactly what I'm feeling and I know exactly what the audience is feeling – and we both want the feeling to grow higher and higher.

This feeling is hard to describe, but it's one I'll remember forever. The best performers in the entertainment or sports field are those who have the special ability to transmit the energy from themselves to the audience. They're good even when not at their peak, but when at their peak - they're truly great!   - Robert Martinez

---

My peak experience will stand out in my mind as long as I live. I had written a song and everybody, including my music teacher, liked it. I was asked to play (piano) and sing this song at our high school graduation.

I don't know if I would want to live it over again because I was so nervous, but I would love to again hear and see the parents

cheering and applauding. The best part was to see both my parents with tears of pride streaming down their faces.
I had a feeling of success and gratitude that was the highest point of my life.

- Herb Laturneau

Why and how does music have this powerful effect on us? The authors of the 2002 Natural Highs, Hyla Cass, M.D. and Patrick Holford, succinctly explain many of the findings of modern science. "Science has developed an extensive body of research that has measured and validated the psychological and physiological benefits of music on human development and behavior....The most powerful effect of music is our physical response to 'the beat'. The phenomenon known as *rhythm entrainment* describes how an external rhythmic stimulus, such as a ticking clock, drum, or pulse in a musical composition, involuntarily causes your heartbeat to match its speed". (p. 268)

(Another example): "the electromagnetic field surrounding our head literally entrains and attunes to the basic electromagnetic field of the earth itself in a state of deep relaxation or meditation. The earth's harmonic resonance has been measured at approximately 8 cycles per second, or 8 hertz (Hz). The frequency range of the electrical activity of the brain that we access in states of deep relaxation is also centered around 8 HZ. ...Music has the power to restore our connection to our essence and with the cosmos." (p. 268)

I have been concerned with the creation of music for more than thirty years, with no lessening of my sense of humility before the majesty of music's expressive power, before its capacity to make manifest a deeply spiritual resource of mankind.

– Aaron Copland

As we leave this section on music, it is clear how powerful a stimulus to PEs is music in its various forms. Since one of the purposes of this book is to exhort and encourage you to foster and nurture peak experiences, a dedication or rededication to listening to – or making - music will be effort well rewarded. We end with wise words of Plato and Aristotle:

> Music is a moral law. It gives a soul to the universe, wings to the mind, flight to the imagination, a charm to sadness, gaiety and life to everything. It is the essence of order, and leads to all that is good, just, and beautiful, of which it is the invisible, but nevertheless dazzling, passionate and eternal form. - Plato
>
> The superior man tries to promote music as a means to the perfection of human culture. When such music prevails, and people's minds are led towards right ideals and aspirations, we may see the appearance of a great nation.
> - Aristotle

SPORTS PERFORMANCE

One very ripe area for peak experiences is sports performance. Mountain-top experiences seem to favor the all-out exertion and focused attention of the athlete. From "runners' high" to athletes being "in the flow" or "in the zone", most sports enthusiasts, or even TV observers, are familiar with the awe-moments that frequently are involved with games and other competitive sports contests.

———

Bill Russell, Basketball Star – "As High As a Skyhawk"

Bill Russell is one of the greatest basketball players of all time. For 13 years he starred with the Boston Celtics.He was a five-time winner of the NBA Most Valuable Player Award. In his 1979 book, <u>Second Wind</u>, we find this description of magic moments on the court.

> Every so often a Celtic game would heat up so that it be-came more than a physical or even a mental game, and would be magical. That feeling is difficult to describe. When it happened, I could feel my play rise to a new level. It came rarely and would last anywhere from five minutes to a whole quarter or more. It would surround not only me and the other Celtics but also the players on the other team and even the referees.

> At that special level, all sorts of odd things happened. The game would be in a white heat of competition, and yet somehow I wouldn't feel competitive – which is a miracle in itself. I'd be putting out the maximum, straining, coughing up parts of my lungs as we ran, and yet I never felt the pain. The game would move so quickly that every fake, cut and pass would be surprising, yet nothing could surprise me. It was almost as if we were playing in slow motion.

> During those spells, I could almost sense how the next play would develop and where the next shot would be taken. Even before the other team brought the ball in bounds, I could feel it so keenly that I'd want to shout to my team-mates, 'It's coming there' - except that I knew that every-thing would change if I did.

> My premonitions would be consistently correct, and I al-ways felt then that I not only knew all the Celtics by heart, but also all the opposing players, and that they all knew me. There have been many times in my career when I felt moved or joyful, but these were the moments when I had chills pulsing up and down my spine.

Sometimes the feeling would last all the way to the end of the game. On the five or 10 occasions when the game ended at that special level, I literally did not care who had won. If we lost, I'd still be as free and high as a skyhawk.
– from <u>Second Wind: the Memories of an Opinionated Man</u>

————

Sports performance peaks are certainly not confined to professional or even great athletes. In this student example, Grace Darnell, writing in her early twenties, tells of a wonderful experience that includes an out-of-body component.

I had for years wanted to learn to water ski; last summer I finally got my chance. My husband and I went to the lake with relatives to water ski. When it came to my turn, the knots of nervousness almost caused me to back down, but I didn't.

I jumped into the cold water and clumsily put on the skis. When I waved my hand as the ready signal, I could feel my body moving through the water. I went faster and faster until I was forced to stand. *There I was skiing and it was like I was sitting in the back of the boat watching "me" ski! There was nobody except "me" skiing and "me" watching me ski. It seemed the only praise I needed was from myself to prove that I could do it. It seemed like forever that I was skiing, when actually it was only about five minutes.*

As soon as "I", the skier, hit the water face first, "I", the watcher, vanished.

————

Quality performance of any kind requires attention and focus of a high order. Later, in Chapter 7 we will speak of "the robot", that part of our mind that takes over the routines of our life and is the enemy of PEs. The robot is left behind in the mountain-top moments of life. This example is from a 19 year old student football player.

> *It would seem like I was walled off from my other feelings and great concentration would take over my consciousness.* For instance, once while playing in a football game, I would be standing in the huddle listening to the play being called – a pass play to me. We'd break from the huddle and approach the line of scrimmage. I could hear the quarterback calling the signals. *As soon as I started running it seemed that I lost all sensation around me. The ball would travel through the silent air and hit my hands. The concentration was incredible. Then, as the play ended, the feelings and senses would slowly return. The sound of the crowd than faded in as if someone were turning up the volume.*
>
> Danny Humpartzoomian

The particular form of activity, whether in sports or not, doesn't seem to matter. Student John Anderson, in his 20s, remembers a golfing PE.

> There was a time last summer when I was playing golf when I felt that I could do no wrong. I usually shoot between 90 and 100 for eighteen holes, but on this particular day I shot a magnificent 80. *I felt before I hit the ball that every shot was going to go where I wanted it to go. Even if I hit the ball wrong, it still ended up on the green by getting a lucky bounce or something. And while I was putting, it was as if my ball was made of iron and each hole was a giant magnet.*

<u>SUMMARY OF CHAPTER THREE</u>   *Music and music performance perform two important functions for human beings. First, rhythm has great binding power to bring us together in communal relationships, as every society's military march music attests. Secondly, as it affects us individually, music can be a powerful stimulant and/or an effective 'soother of the savage beast.' It can increase our productivity, uplift our sense of well-being and often take us to the heights of ecstasy. It is second only to nature as a stimulus to peak experiences.*

Performance, whether on the stage or on the playing field, because it requires complete commitment and concentration, frequently is the occasion for our "going out of ourselves", one of the descriptions of PEs.

In the next chapter, we will examine a dozen transcendent experiences that have not only changed the individual 'peakers', but also affected, often in profoundly important ways, all of us, and all of human history.

Chapter Four

PEAK EXPERIENCES THAT CHANGE LIVES AND WORLDS

On the physical level, the human race and the earth appear to change very slowly. Except for extraordinary, cataclysmic events such as earthquakes involving great tsunamis, or falling meteors, evolutionary change requires extended periods, eons of time.

On cultural and historical levels, however, human change and development often occur with relative speed. *It is the thesis of this book that, most often, significant cultural changes and developments occur as the result of peak experiences, mountain top moments, that happen to individuals while in an alternate state of consciousness.*

Very often, a PE is a watershed event, so moving and powerful that life cannot be the same after the experience. Even a cursory review of history points to the importance of such events – for the whole race as well as for the individuals involved. *For the most part, the human race changes only as a result of the changes of certain self-actualized individuals who have themselves changed after undergoing extraordinary moments of enlightenment.*

Just as children go through "growth spurts" as their bodies mature, so do individuals exhibit "mind spurts" which, in turn, seed the whole race's development. All such change is the evolutionary process at work. We humans are in this way fulfilling our destiny which is basically to reach for the constantly expanding "farther reaches of human nature." It is another way of understanding that time-honored phrase – 'reaching for the stars'.

FOUR FAMOUS EXAMPLES OF WORLD CHANGING PEAKS

In every field of human endeavor – the arts and music; farming and industry; religion and philosophy; science and mechanics – great milestones of progress have been the results of PEs, extraordinary "AHA moments" of insight and clarity in the lives of individuals.

Four brief examples will illustrate this point – four well known persons who changed the world with their work inspired by their peak moments of insight: an inventor, an author, a composer and a scientist.

INVENTOR ELIAS HOWE

Many inventors, who have contributed mightily to the ongoing Industrial Revolution, often attribute their breakthrough ideas to dreams which solved vexing problems for them. Dreams, of course, fit our template of altered states of consciousness. Consider, for example, Elias Howe, the inventor of the sewing machine, which, of course, spawned a whole new industry. He reported that he couldn't figure out how to thread a rapidly moving needle. The answer came in a dream with menacing cannibals dancing around a pot in which Howe and his companions were to be cooked for dinner. When Howe looked closely at the spears, he noticed a circular hole near the tip of each spear. Upon waking, he immediately knew his problem was solved. Prior to this, the thread followed at the far end of the needle. Having the hole at the top of the needle solved many problems with the new machine.

AUTHOR ROBERT LOUIS STEVENSON

Authors, too, often relate receiving similar help from "outside sources" (though we contend that the sources are not outside of us, but are unrecognized aspects of our normal human capabilities). Robert Lewis Stevenson spoke of his "Brownies" who assisted him periodically with ideas, In fact, he related that one of his most famous stories, "Dr Jekyll and Mr. Hyde," was given to him intact by his Brownies one night while sleeping. In the morning, he began to write the story, but couldn't remember the ending. So, before going to sleep the next night, he asked for the ending and was relieved the next morning to realize that the ending had been given to him by the Brownies.

COMPOSER JOHANNES BRAHMS

In the realm of music, it is well known that many of the great composers, including Mozart, Bach and Brahms, attested that they were not really the composers of their work but merely the channels through which the music came from the celestial sources. Johannes Brahms reported, "Straightway the ideas flow in upon me, directly from God, and not only do I see distinct themes in my mind's eye, but they are clothed in the right forms, harmonies and orchestration. Measure by measure, the finished product is revealed to me when I am in those rare, inspired moods."

SCIENTIST ALBERT EINSTEIN

And even in science, ofttimes we are told that the most remarkable and world-changing ideas give up their secrets when the scientist is in another frame of reference, another state of consciousness. Among many possible examples, we have chosen this about Albert Einstein, perhaps the greatest scientific genius of the last millennium. We are indebted to Dawson Church for this excerpt from his 2007 The Genie in Your Genes.

One evening, Albert Einstein's son-in-law, Dmitri Marianoff, sat with him in a house in Berlin, Germany, after all the other members of the family had gone to bed. Into the pregnant stillness, Marianoff asked a question that had long intrigued him:

'How is it, Albert, that you arrived at your theory?

'In a vision', he answered.

He said that one night he had gone to bed with a discouragement of such black depths that no argument would pierce it. 'When one's thoughts fall into despair, nothing serves him any longer, not his hours of work, not his past successes – nothing. All reassurance is gone. It is finished, I told myself, it is useless. There are no results. I must give it up.'

Then this happened. With infinite precision the universe with its underlying unity of size, structure, distance, time, space, slowly fell piece by piece, like a monolithic picture puzzle, into place in Albert Einstein's mind. Suddenly clear, like a giant die that made an indelible impress, a huge map of the universe outlined itself in one clarified vision.

'And that is when peace came, and that is when conviction came, and with these things came an almighty calm that nothing could ever shake again...'

The creative flowering of consciousness is as mysterious as Einstein's vision. After he had that insight, it then took him another four years to work out his seminal equations showing the link between energy and matter. But the first impulse was a gift from the universe, seeding a mind open to receiving a new way of seeing the cosmos. (pp.199, 200)

AN ECSTASY OF UNITY — Astronaut Edgar Mitchell

Astronaut, scientist, author, lecturer Edgar Mitchell, while returning from the moon aboard Apollo 14, had the experience that changed his life as he looked down on earth through space. Excerpts for his writings about this event follow.

There was a vast tranquility, a growing sense of wonder as I looked out the window....Somehow I felt tuned into something much larger than myself, something much larger than the planet in the window. Something incomprehensibly big...looking beyond the earth itself to the magnificence of the larger scene, there was a startling recognition that the nature of the universe was not as I had been taught. *In a peak experience, the presence of divinity became almost palpable and I* knew *that life in the universe was not just an accident based on random processes. This knowledge came to me directly – noetically...Clearly the universe had meaning and direction...*

There was an upwelling of fresh insight coupled with a feeling of ubiquitous harmony – a sense of interconnectedness with the celestial bodies surrounding our spacecraft...This wasn't a 'religious' or otherworldly experience...it was just a pointer, a signpost showing the direction toward new viewpoints and greater understanding...This new feeling was illusive, its full meaning somehow obscured, but its silent authority shook me to the very core... *I experienced what has been described as an ecstasy of unity. I not only saw the connectedness, I felt it and experienced it sentiently.* (From <u>The Way of the Explorer and Psychic Exploration</u>, p. 29) (Italics added)

Dr. Edgar Mitchell co-founded IONS, the Institute of Noetic Sciences in 1973, two years after his life-changing NASA trip in space and walking on the moon. IONS encourages, funds, and conducts scientific research on human potentials. Its mission: Advancing the science of consciousness and human experience to serve individual and collective transformation.

————

TEACHER-TO-BE

Very often peak experiences provide absolutely clear guidance leading recipients to a particular vocation. The following is from a college student written when she was in her twenties. It is not surprising that Jean did, indeed, become a teacher.

Ever since first grade when I was chosen to explain a lesson to a classmate who had been absent, I've wanted to be a teacher. My first grade teacher, Mrs. Stiner, was a wonderful teacher and a great inspiration to me.

For the past two summers I have worked as a teaching assistant at an elementary school. For a week last year the regular teacher was out of town. A substitute teacher was called in and, since she was unfamiliar with some of the activities, I got to teach certain of the lessons. *While I was teaching and 28 pairs of eyes were glued on me, I was no longer Jean, the teacher's assistant; I was my first grade teacher, Mrs. Stiner. For a while I felt, and even sounded, like her. It was as if we were one person, she and I, imparting knowledge to those children.*

I am truly grateful to her for providing me a positive role model to help me realize my purpose for being.

– Jean Converse

PRISON PEAK EXPERIENCE OF ANWAR el-SADAT-
A STEP TOWARD PEACE IN THE MIDDLE EAST

Prisons have sometimes been the trigger for life changing and world changing PEs. One striking example from recent history is Anwar Sadat of Egypt. Sadat was a leading figure in modern Egypt for many decades. He served as third President from 1970 until his death in 1981. He was awarded the Nobel Peace Prize after successfully negotiating, with Israeli Prime Minister Begin, the Egyptian-Israeli Peace Treaty in 1979.

In his autobiography, Sadat looked back fondly on the days he spent in Cell 54 though conditions there were extremely rigorous and difficult.

Now in the complete solitude of Cell 54, when I had no links at all with the outside world...the only way in which I could break my loneliness was, paradoxically, to seek the companionship of that inner entity I call 'self'...

Once released from the narrow confines of the 'self,', with its mundane suffering and petty emotions, a man will have

stepped into a new, undiscovered world which is vaster
and richer, uniting with existence in its entirety, transcend-
ing time and space. Through this process of liberation, the
human will develops into a love-force, and all earthly forces...come to contribute to the achievement of perfect inner
peace, and so provide a man with absolute happiness....
It was genuinely a conquest, for *in that world I came to
experience friendship with God....My friendship with God
changed me a great deal. Only in defense of a just cause
would I take up arms...*

It was in Cell 54 that I discovered that love is truly the key
to everything. When the heavy shackles that had bound me
to my 'narrow self' were removed, I began to enjoy God's
love. I felt I lived in His love, that love was a law of life. In
love, life – nay, being itself – becomes possible; without
love, being comes to an end.

When *my individual entity merged into the vaster entity of
all existence*, my point of departure became love of home
(Egypt), love of all being, love of God..
I regard my last eight months in prison as the happiest time
of my life. It was then that I was initiated into that new world
of self-abnegation which enabled my soul to merge into all
other beings, to expand and establish communion with the
Lord of all Being.
- <u>In Search of Identity: An autobiography</u>, pp.18, 85-87.
(Italics added)

A MAGIC MOMENT IN THE MEADOW – LIFE AS CELEBRATION

This book is dedicated to Thomas Berry, a man who had a magic
moment in a meadow which changed and shaped his own life and

the lives of many others, including the author's. He was only eleven years old at the time. His family had just moved to a newly built house at the edge of a Southern town. The house was situated on a slight incline; down below was a small creek and across the creek was a meadow.

It was an early afternoon in May when I first looked down over the scene and saw the meadow. The field was covered with lilies rising above the thick grass. *A magic moment, this experience gave to my life something, I know not what, that seems to explain my life at a more profound level that almost any other experience I can remember.*

...as the years pass, this moment returns to me, and whenever I think about my basic life attitude and the whole trend of my mind and causes I have given my efforts to, *I seem to come back to this moment and the impact it had on my feeling for what is real and worthwhile in life.*

This early experience, it seems, has become normative for me throughout the range of my thinking. Whatever preserves and enhances this meadow in the natural cycle of its transformation is good; what is opposed to this meadow or negates it is not good. My life orientation is that simple. It is also that pervasive. It applies in economics and political orientation as well as in education and religion and whatever.

...Religion too, it seems to me, takes it origin here in the deep mystery of this setting. The more a person thinks of the infinite number of interrelated activities taking place here, the more mysterious it all becomes, the more meaning a person finds in the Maytime blooming of the lilies, the more awestruck a person might be in simply looking over this little patch of meadowland. It had none of the maj-

esty of the Appalachian or the Western mountains, none of the immensity or the power of oceans, nor even the harsh magnificence of desert country; yet *in this little meadow the magnificence of life as celebration is manifested in a manner as profound and as impressive as any other place that I have known in these past many years.*
The Great Work, pp. 12-13 (Italics added)

Thomas Berry went on to write books and articles that influenced many thousands to take a serious view of what we humans were doing to our the earth heritage. Interested readers are referred to the bibliography.

Origin moments are supremely important. – Thomas Berry

REALIZATION IN A PARKING LOT

Life changing experiences need not always happen as moments of intense bliss (sometimes referred to as the Fireworks Effect). Sometimes they are just relatively quiet moments of deep knowing. By their fruits we shall know whether or not they are, indeed, life changing. A seventy-five year old woman relates this parking lot event that happened many years ago and the profound effect it has had on her life ever since.

Like all young people perhaps, I remember feeling that others I observed seemed to be a lot more confident and sure of themselves than I was. The internal fears and struggles that I felt seemed to be happening only to me. For a short time after college and before my marriage I was working in the local library. One day as I stepped into the parking lot, *it*

suddenly came to me that everyone is frightened some of the time. A huge feeling of understanding and relief came over me. I can still picture where I was standing in the warm sunshine.

It is very important that I am clear about what this meant to my life. It was the beginning of any compassion I am able to summon. That very simple realization was also crucial to whatever understanding of the human condition I've been able to find in what is now 75 years of experience in the world. Goodness knows that I've not overcome a tendency to be overly critical and sometimes dismissive of others, but I will always know that fear is a part of life and that I am not alone. — **Colleen Kitzmiller Holmbeck**

A DRUG INDUCED VISION OF LIGHT –DR. STANISLAV GROF

After graduating from medical school and while a psychiatric resident in a Czecholovakian hospital, young Doctor Stanislav Grof volunteered for an experiment with LSD and altered states. This event was to change the entire life of this man who was to become one of the world's best known and most respected researchers of human consciousness.

LSD, the powerful psychoactive drug, had been discovered by chemist Albert Hofmann in Basel, Switzerland, in 1943. Dr. Grof had already been an observer at many sessions of Czech clinical experiments. "My appetite had been repeatedly whetted by fantastic accounts of the experiences of others that I had witnessed."

Grof describes this, his first direct experience with LSD-induced altered states in the fall of 1956 as, "without a doubt, the single most important and influential experience of my entire life." He describes this event in his 2009 book, <u>When the Impossible Happens: Adventures in Non-Ordinary Realities.</u>

I had an overwhelming and indescribable experience of cosmic consciousness...At one point when a giant stroboscopic light above my head was turned on, I was hit by a vision of incredible radiance and supernatural beauty. It made me think of the accounts of mystical experience I had read about in spiritual literature, in which the visions of divine light were compared with the incandescence of millions of suns.

I felt that a divine thunderbolt had catapulted my conscious self out of my body. I lost my awareness of the research assistant, the laboratory, the psychiatric clinic, Prague, and then the planet. My consciousness expanded at an inconceivable speed and reached cosmic dimensions. There were no more boundaries or difference between me and the universe....I found myself at the center of a cosmic drama of unimaginable dimensions....

This day marked the beginning of my radical departure from traditional thinking in psychiatry and from the monistic materialism of Western science. ...Not believing at the time, as I do today, that the potential for a mystical experience is the natural birthright of all human beings, I attributed everything to the effect of LSD. ...

And right there and then, I decided to dedicate my life to the study of non-ordinary states of consciousness. (Prologue –pp. xxxiii – xxxv)

When the use of LSD was legally suppressed in the late 1960s, Grof went on to discover that many of these states of mind could be explored without drugs. He developed one particular breathing technique which became known as "Holotropic Breathwork" which is still taught and used very successfully today.

Stanislav Grof remains a leader in the field of consciousness research. One of the founders of the field of transpersonal psychology, he has received many prestigious awards for raising consciousness of transpersonal realities in the scientific community. His life changing experience in 1956 resulted in impressive forward thrusts for him and for the world.

THE PEAK EXPERIENCE BIRTH OF ALCOHOLICS ANONYMOUS

It is well known by the more than a million AA members and former members that the origin of their organization was a peak experience that occurred on the worst night of founder Bill Wilson's life, December 14, 1934. The 39 year old Wilson, a broken down drunk, was 'drying out' – for the fourth time – at a detox center in Manhattan. While there, he received a visit from an old drinking buddy, Ebby Thatcher, who had recently found religion and given up alcohol.

Thatcher pleaded with Wilson to do likewise. "Realize you are licked, admit it, and get willing to turn your life over to God," Thatcher counseled his desperate friend. Wilson, a confirmed agnostic, gagged at the thought of asking a supernatural being for help.

But later, as he writhed in his hospital bed, still heavily under the influence of belladonna, Wilson decided to give God a try. "If there is a God, let Him show Himself!" he cried out. "I am ready to do anything. Anything!"

What happened next is an essential piece of AA lore: A white light filled Wilson's hospital room, and God revealed himself to the shattered stockbroker. *"It seemed to me, in the mind's eye, that I was on a mountain and that a wind,*

> ***not of air but of spirit, was blowing," he later said. "And
> then it burst upon me that I was a free man."** Wilson would
> never drink again.*
>   **- Koerner, "Secret of AA" p. 131   (Italics added.)**

Within six months of Wilson's mountain-top experience, he met
and helped surgeon Robert Smith, "Dr. Bob", overcome his addiction. The date of Dr. Bob's surrender, June 10, 1935, became the
founding date for Alcoholics Anonymous.

PEACE PILGRIM – HOW DID IT START?

Peace Pilgrim, whose birth name (which she never used in her
walking years) was Mildred Norman, was a woman who walked
across the United States seven times. She started during the Korean War and continued walking and witnessing for peace for 28
years until her untimely death in a traffic accident in 1981. She was
a pilgrim for peace, talking peace wherever she went, most often
at churches, universities, and local radio and television stations.
Her only possessions were the clothes on her back and a few items
she carried in her tunic pockets. She had no formal organizational
backing, carried no money and would not even ask for food or
shelter.

Peace Pilgrim had an enormous following. An all-volunteer
non-profit organization published and distributed over 400,000
copies of her book and half a million copies of her booklet, Steps
Toward Inner Peace. She was a spiritual presence and a teacher by
example; she touched many lives in profound ways.

She is a fine example of the thousands of persons who receive
the knowledge of their life's purpose through a peak experience.
She tells about it in these excerpts from her book, Peace Pilgrim:
Her Life and Work in Her Own Words.

There were hills and valleys, lots of hills and valleys, in my spiritual growing up period. Then in the midst of the struggle there came a wonderful mountaintop experience – the first glimpse of what the life of inner peace was like....

That came when I was out walking in the early morning. All of a sudden I felt very uplifted, more uplifted than I had ever been. I remember I knew *timelessness* and *spacelessness* and *lightness*. I did not seem to be walking on the earth. There were no people or even animals around, but every flower, every bush, every tree, seemed to wear a halo. There was a light emanation around everything. Flecks of gold fell like slanted rain through the air....

The most important part of it was not the phenomena, but the realization of the oneness of all creation, not only human beings ... but all the creatures and most wonderful of all, a oneness with that which permeates all and binds all together and gives life to all. A oneness with that which many would call God.... I have never felt separate since....

The inspiration for the pilgrimage came at this time. ...I saw, in my mind's eye, myself walking along and wearing the garb of my mission....I saw a map of the United States with the large cities marked – and it was as though someone had taken a colored crayon and marked a zigzag line across, coast to coast and border to border, from Los Angeles to New York City. *I knew what I was to do.* And that was a vision of my first year's pilgrimage route in 1953!

I entered a new and wonderful world. My life was blessed with a meaningful purpose. (Italics added) (pp. 21,22)

SUMMARY OF CHAPTER FOUR   *In this chapter we have seen twelve examples of persons whose lives have been changed in profound ways through extraordinary and deeply moving experiences. After one such experience, the rest of one's life is significantly changed. And, in each case, the "ripple effect" on the rest of the world has been significant. Some PEs, like Albert Einstein's, result in highly publicized world changes. All PEs affect each peakee's life and all those he or she contacts after the event– which is another way of saying that each of us affects the larger world whether we are aware of it or not.*

In the next section we will consider the children, the young and the young-at-heart. We will see that PEs come very early to some and that profound events can often be childlike, even. whimsical, in nature.

CHAPTER FIVE

THE YOUNG AND THE YOUNG AT HEART

Some people believe that children, pure and fresh and new, are closer to the Source – whether the Source is seen as Higher Self, God, Nature, the Universe, etc. – than adults can be. However one explains it, children often appear to be in altered state of consciousness and their tales of "unusual" experiences are very common. Many adults attribute these reports of the children to nothing more than signs of vivid imaginations not yet jaded by maturity and the 'real world'. But, as has been often suggested by poets and seers, perhaps the magical world of childhood is more real that the limited outlook of the left-brain adult society. This has been beautifully expressed by former Poet Laureate of the United States, Billy Collins, in his poem "On Turning Ten."

On Turning Ten

The whole idea of it makes me feel
like I'm coming down with something,
something worse than any stomach ache
or the headaches I get from reading in bad light –
a kind of measles of the spirit
a mumps of the psyche,
a disfiguring of the soul.

You tell me it is too early to be looking back,
but that is because you have forgotten
the perfect simplicity of being one
and the beautiful complexity introduced by two.
But I can lie on my bed and remember every digit.
At four I was an Arabian wizard.
I could make myself invisible
by drinking a glass of milk a certain way.
At seven I was a soldier, at nine a prince.

But now I am mostly at the window
watching the late afternoon light.
Back then it never fell so solemnly
against the side of my tree house,
and my bicycle never leaned against the garage
as it does today,
All the dark blue speed drained out of it.

This is the beginning of sadness, I say to myself,
as I walk through the universe in my sneakers.
It is time to say good-bye to my imaginary friends,
time to turn the first big number.

Il seems only yesterday I used to believe
there was nothing under my skin but light.

If you cut me I would shine.
But now when I fall upon the sidewalks of life,
I skin my knees. I bleed.

(From <u>Sailing Around the Room</u>)

Part of the mission of this book is to increase the awareness among adults that PE's are to be expected among children and, unless the child has trouble distinguishing the fanciful and the real, it would be wise to encourage children to talk about these occurrences, to accept them as natural. One is reminded that among Abraham Maslow's college students, the incidences of PEs increased as the students reported and discussed them in classes.

The examples cited in this chapter are usually from adults who are remembering events from their childhoods, and also from childlike adults who seem to have recaptured, or perhaps never lost, the openness and freedom of children.

SUCCESSFULLY PLANTED

Dr. Elmer Green (b.1917) is best known today as the Father of Clinical Biofeedback and the founder of the Voluntary Controls Program at the Menniger Clinic. He and his late wife, Alyce Green, were pioneers in the integration of subtle-energies and energy-medicine concepts with theory and research in Western science and technology. He was a founder of both ISSSEEM, The International Society for the Study of Subtle Energies and Energy Medicine, and of the Association of Applied Psychophysiology and Biofeedback.

In his ground-breaking autobiography, <u>The Ozawkie Book of the Dead: Alzheimer's Isn't</u> <u>What You Think It Is</u>, Green tells the beautiful love story of his caring for Alyce during the last seven years of her life while she had Alzheimer's. (She died in 1994). Among hundreds of altered state experiences explored in the book, Green recalls that "a striking event occurred when I was three years old which created *the most vivid and indelible memory of my life* – and even today, it seems as bright as when it happened."

I was sitting in one of those old stuffed-leather armchairs with my back up against one side, my right shoulder somewhat turned against the back of the chair, and my feet straight across the seat, not quite touching the other side. What a comfortable chair, I thought, And then I remembered thinking, with great self-awareness, 'This isn't such a bad place after all.'

That thought had hardly crossed my mind when the opposite wall of the room began to brighten with a golden hue, and as the gold increased in intensity, the curtains over the windows, and the windows, too, and all the furniture of the room, vanished. How surprising – and interesting. I'd never before seen such a thing. Even the ceiling and hanging light fixture disappeared in the gold light.

As I gazed in wonderment at this transformation, I became aware that about 100 feet away, beyond the upper corner of the room, which was approximately 30 degrees up and a little to my left, a group of men were gliding toward me. They were dressed in shining soft-white belted robes. In a few seconds they arrived in the golden room and stopped a few feet away. The leader was a tall figure with a black beard. He wore a white turban or long headgear of some kind that came down to his shoulders along his cheekbones. A circular band of material held it in place on his forehead.

Looking down at me, he smiled, and said some words that have remained forever engraved in my mind, *'We are here. You are there. And you have been successfully planted.'* Astonished, I said nothing. Merely watched as the group and the golden light slowly faded, and curtains, windows, and walls reappeared.

That event produced a deep knowing in me that: 1)Other worlds existed. 2) They were populated. 3) People there were concerned with what happened on Earth. Also, I knew, deeply, that I 'belonged' to an enterprise of some kind, and would have something to do.

Following that experience, years passed without a single additional occurrence of that kind. In other words, *I was planted*, and then allowed to grow up in a normal way, suffering the pangs and tribulation, and joys of my karma, learning to live in the world like every person. During those growing-up years, however, the above event remained vivid in my memory as an experience-that-underlay-everything, even though I didn't 'think' about it....(pp. 258,259)

Here is an account of a mystical experience that came unbidden to sixteen year old Andrew Cohen, who went on to become a leading scholar and author on evolutionary spirituality and founder of Enlighten/Next magazine.

When I was sixteen, I had an experience of cosmic consciousness that occurred spontaneously. Completely unsought, it emerged from the unknown. I was sitting up late one evening speaking with someone and suddenly, for no apparent reason, the doors of perception opened....

I saw in a way that is difficult to put into words that all of life is One – that the whole universe and everything that exists within it, seen and unseen, known and unknown, is one conscious, intelligent Being, that is self-aware. Its nature is Love but it is Love that is so overwhelming in its intensity that even to experience the faintest hint of it is almost unbearable for the human body. I saw in that moment that there is no such thing as death, that life has no beginning and no end. I was awestruck and overwhelmed. Tears were rolling down my cheek and yet I wasn't crying…. And then, something curious happened – I don't exactly know how to explain it. There was a message for me that said: "If you give your life to me and me alone, you'll have nothing to fear."…

I had no particular religious conviction at that point because I had been brought up an atheist, but I was obviously impacted by this unexpected revelation. In those few moments, I had been in touch with something that was utterly real. Infinitely more real than anything I had ever experienced before. As a matter of fact, it seemed as if I had been dead my whole life in contrast with the event that had just occurred. For that brief period I was awake; I was truly alive for the first time. This I know without any doubt.– Cohen, Living Enlightenment, pp.31-32)

AN EIGHT YEAR OLD'S MOVING MOVIE EXPERIENCE

The following early life-changing experience is reported by a well known photographer, David Vandre, whose photography studio is in Hendersonville, North Carolina.

I was just eight years old in 1950 when I saw the film, "The Third Man". My parents were visiting friends in Berkeley, California. Knowing that it would be boring for an 8 year old to be with a bunch of adults drinking beer, smoking and talking all afternoon, they gave me money and sent me around the corner to the movies. (In those days it was safe and not that unusual for a kid to go to the movies alone, and films weren't rated.)

I found myself watching one of the classic film noirs of all time. "The Third Man" was set in rubble-strewn post-war Vienna and, like most film noir movies, much of it was shot at night. At 8 years old, the film's focus on the four-power occupation of Vienna and black market activities wasn't something I understood. However, *I found myself fascinated with the incredible noir imagery, especially the tilted angles and creative compositions.*

"The Third Man" really changed my life. From that time on I found myself as interested in the process of movie photography as the story. I became a life long movie buff, interested in how movies are made, and I have made films myself. Although I have concentrated on still photography for the past 25 years, I often shoot a series of stills of a subject as if it were a movie sequence.

Ever since that early visit to "The Third Man", I have responded to the world with creative activity. Since childhood I have been active drawing, singing and acting, but photography is my one great, continuing passion. I constantly think about how to improve my vision for compelling images and to expand my skills in conveying them to others, both through capturing the image in the camera and through creative editing.

The following experience of thirteen year Carly Newfeld speaks of the problem of ignorant, small-minded adults who tend to stifle the spirit of youngsters who are more aware of other dimensions of reality than the adults in question. Carly, even though thwarted by her English teacher, went on to become an author. This excerpt, detailing two peak experiences, is from one of her books.

While walking in the hills near my home on December 24, 1961, I spontaneously experienced an illumination of all knowing, transcendent, loving, Divine Consciousness. I was thirteen years old. Returning to school after the Christmas break, we were asked to write an essay about our holiday. I wrote two pages about my experience and excitedly gave it to my teacher, hoping I would receive an 'A' for such an inspiring and good piece of writing.

Two days later, my essay was returned marked "see me" in red ink, and the teacher sternly called me up in front of the class. She asked me from where I had copied such profane "drivel", accused me of lying when I insisted on the truth, and finally threw my essay in the rubbish bin. Faced with humiliation and disappointment, I momentarily withered. Then, as I walked back to my desk, a lightening bolt of clarity hit me and I realized that I would dedicate my life to proving that what I experienced on the hill was real, and that I would guide others to find the loving divinity within, their authentic voice, and the courage to speak. This book is one small piece of the inner commitment I made that day in school. (Newfeld, <u>The Findhorn Book of Guidance and Intuition</u>, p. 125)

Confirmed For Life at Age Twelve

When I was twelve years old, I was confirmed into the Episcopal Church. I remember kneeling at the altar, or at least at the front of the sanctuary where communion was performed. When our pastor placed his hand on the top of my head and began his recitation, I was overcome with a feeling of warmth and euphoria that I hadn't experienced before. I haven't experienced it since, either. I'm not sure words can adequately describe the feeling, but I remember a "glow" that totally surrounded and permeated my body and my soul. I felt like a powerful voice was saying "Welcome" and that I was being smiled upon. It was an overwhelming feeling of complete acceptance and love and it deeply affected me.

I think about it every so often. Whenever I have doubts about whether there's a God, I seek comfort in remembering that I, for that brief moment, encountered a presence that can only be God.

- Thomas Hedrick

OLDER IN BODY BUT STILL YOUNG AT HEART
A FRISBEE STORY

Immediately upon thinking about peak experiences, I reveled in a vivid memory from nearly 20 years ago. Amazingly, when I asked my wife to think about a peak experience, she remembered the same event.

The scene was Oak Park, Illinois. Michele and I have our first apartment while she attends medical school and I work on my English doctorate. Life is good, but we are certainly under a variety of pressures, e.g. academic, financial, and even emotional as a young couple living away from our families for the first time.

One of the ways we relax is by visiting the local park just a few blocks away. We have always enjoyed throwing the Frisbee to each other, so that is what we do today. As we sling the disc back and forth, we joyfully repeat the motions of our courtship when I would try to impress her with my trick catches and she would try to impress me with her effortless accuracy. Now that we no longer need to impress each other, it is just plain fun to play catch.

Gradually, though, clouds start to roll in and it looks like we'll have to go back to the apartment soon.

Then something unexpected happens; – it starts to sprinkle, and we just keep playing Frisbee. Then it starts to rain harder, but we just keep playing. We both assume the other is about to end the game, but neither does! So we play on, and get wet, and slip all over the grass, and laugh, and smile, and laugh some more!

This goes on for at least twenty minutes before we finally run for cover beneath a nearby tree as the downpour continues. But we are so wet already, it really doesn't matter how much more rain comes down. We just look at each other with smiling eyes.

In hindsight, we both can see that our time in the rain was a wonderful release from the pressures of our lives back then. It was so liberating to be outside the control of adult obligation.

Even more important, however, is another wonder of hindsight. For now we can see that our shared peak experience on that otherwise normal day in Chicagoland solidified our relationship at a crucial moment in our history. Even after all these years, it is quickly recalled because it is central to our identity as a couple.

Whoever thought that a simple game of catch could be such a deep kind of intimacy? Decades later, Michele and I still play catch through all kinds of weather.

— Vincent O'Keefe

A Timeless Space Without Edges

When I was about ten years old, I remember one summer day, lying on my back looking up at the sky and imagining the configuration of clouds as people, animals, angels, and so on. Then for some reason, I started thinking about the word 'infinity'. The concept was new to me and I wanted to contemplate it uninterruptedly. *As I lay there, lost in my thoughts, all of a sudden I was lost in the clouds. There was no more 'me', nor clouds, nor anything. The expanse was before, after, above, below, all around, and yet not there at all. It was only for a moment, I suppose, that I felt blended into a timeless space without edges. I came to myself a bit frightened, and yet with a sense of awe.* ...I never told anyone about this experience. I didn't think adults would understand.

- R. Hart

DEVELOPMENTAL PEAK EXPERIENCES

Like adult PEs, not all children's peak experiences seem to us profound and highly significant. Yet, when perceived in terms of the mental and spiritual development of children, many PEs are remembered fondly far into adult life. The following is an example of a developmental PE.

Teeth Marks on the Window Sill

The memories of childhood can often be vague. It wasn't until I was visiting my mother at the home of my childhood that I experienced a feeling of my inner self, or what some call spirit or soul.

My mother had turned my old bedroom into a sewing room. It seemed hard to relate to the sewing room as my old bed-room, maybe because it was so clean! As I sat on the bed and looked around, I noticed some strange markings on the window sill. I got up to get a better look at the sill and saw the teeth marks of a small child still engraved in the wood. *I remembered myself at the age of two sinking my teeth into the soft pine as I gazed out the window. The memory only lasted a few seconds, but the feeling of being the same per-son, whether I was two or twenty-two, still remains deep in-side me.*

- Ellie Godwin, 22 year old college student

FALLING IN LOVE WITH LANGUAGE -A

I (the author) am the father of six children. Among the thrills of parenthood was the experience of watching each child – at various ages between four and seven – fall in love with language. It seems to me, in retrospect, that they were having "experiences of bliss" as they realized – partly all at once and partly over time, progressively – the miracle of language. My kids suddenly seemed more alive. They would read, or attempt to read, anything in sight, including cereal boxes at the breakfast table. They would read, silently or aloud, any print they could find while smiling broad happy grins.

A theatrical event I witnessed in the past speaks to this topic of PEs related to language.

Many years ago, I was privileged to see, on Broadway, the play, "The Miracle Worker" about Helen Keller, featuring the child star, Patty Duke, as Helen, and Anne Bancroft as her teacher, Anne Sullivan.

Helen Keller (1880-1968) was an extraordinary author, political activist and lecturer who, when she was nine months old, had been stricken with an illness that had left her blind and deaf.

There was an electric moment on stage after a very realistic tussle between the unruly and misbehaving seven-year-old Helen and Anne Sullivan. Anne forces Helen to fill a pitcher with water from a well because Helen, in an angry tirade, had deliberately spilled the pitcher.

While the water is splashing over Helen's hand, Anne, always the teacher, uses the sign language alphabet which she has been teaching Helen on Helen's hand, to make the letters W-A-T-E-R. Suddenly Helen becomes rapt with attention, a beautiful smile on her face, as she mumbles her first spoken word in seven years, "wa-wa". The mystery of language has been revealed to her – and her life changes forever.

This highly dramatic depiction of Helen Keller's greatest peak experience is the highlight of the play - and the later film. Many in the audience that night, I'm sure, had their own transcendent moment as we watched these two consummate actresses reenact a powerful, life-changing moment.

FALLING IN LOVE WITH LANGUAGE – B

The first Asian writer to win the Noble prize for Literature, Rabindranath Tagore (1861-1941), is considered one of the world's finest writers of any age. He was thought of as the living embodiment of Indian culture and its greatest spokesman. In this excerpt from My Life, he remembers his own 'falling in love with language':

> **"I remember the day in my childhood when, after the painful process of learning my Bengali alphabet, I unexpectedly came to the first simple combination of letters which gave me the words: 'It rains, the leaves tremble'. I was thrilled with the picture which these words suggested to me. The fragments lost their individual isolation and my mind reveled in the unity of a vision." (quoted in A Tagore Reader, p.86)**

THAT FULL FEELING AGAIN

Teacher/Poet Coleman Barks, well known as the translator of the poetry of the Sufi poet Rumi, was once asked by public television interviewer Bill Moyers about 'ecstasy'. Barks told this story of regular peak moments growing up in the beautiful mountains of Tennessee.

> **When I was seven or eight, and that golden time came in early evening when the sun is getting ready to set, I would fall on the ground and hug myself. I would call to my mama and say, "Mom, I've got that full feeling again." My mom, playing bridge with her neighbors, would say, "Yes, dear."**

I KNEW I WAS GROWING UP AND NO LONGER AFRAID

In the summer of my seventeenth year, when I was still in high school, I used to work at a Waterpark located in downtown Niagara Falls (New York) just a few blocks from the falls itself. By mid-August the college kids who worked there had to quit to go back to college and the only workers left were kids my own age.

On this particular evening, the sun was dripping into the horizon leaving a spectacular array of golds, oranges and reds. Of course, I'd seen lovely sunsets before, but never really stopped everything to take it all in. The colors danced in the sky and seemed to have a third dimension. We all just stood there watching. *No one said anything for quite a few minutes and just stood mesmerized. ...It seemed at that moment that I knew I was growing up, and in a split second, I was no longer afraid of it.*

- Suzanne Birmingham, Student

THE DYING AND THE DEAD

Two young college students reflect on unforgettable transcendent experiences with those who have passed on.

A. LOVE AND PEACE – A CEMETERY EXPERIENCE

One gorgeous sunny afternoon I had just gotten home from school when my girlfriend called and asked me to go to Forest Lawn Cemetery in Buffalo (New York) with her. As morbid as it may sound, I had heard that this cemetery is very special and very beautiful, so I quickly agreed to go.

As we entered through the ornate iron gates, I felt a fore-shadowing of what was to come – a warm , refreshing sensation traveled through my bones. As we walked along we saw many beautiful grave markers, huge statues of angels and soldiers and doves, and there were enormous hand-carved mausoleums scattered throughout. I was amazed and very joyful and, at the same time, a little solemn.

When we turned around, we realized we were surrounded by large hills covered with more graves and monuments. We climbed to the top of the highest hill and I stood there staring into the powerful beams of the late afternoon sun-light. *I was overcome with a feeling of love and peace that was totally indescribable.* Below us was a small pond. The sun reflected off the silky surface of the water and from the down of the many swans, geese and ducks. *It was an incredible experience that I will never forget.*

– Student Diane Avino

B. GRANDPA SPOKE MY NAME

When I reflect back to one moment in my life that I would like to relive, it would have to be the day before my grand-father died. In was in early June of 1977; I was eleven years old. We were over to Gram's for our usual Sunday dinner, but that day something seemed different to me. I had a strange feeling.

My brother, Vince, and I walked to the ice cream parlor down the street to buy lemon ice and ice cream for the fam-ily. Mom said I could feed Grandpa some ice cream. Some-one always had to feed him because, as a result of multiple strokes, he was paralyzed. He had not been able to speak for the fifteen years since the first stroke.

I was alone with Grandpa, sitting in the parlor giving him spoonfuls of lemon ice, chattering to him as I did so. Suddenly, he spoke my name, "Beth"! He told me he loved me and urged me to always be a good girl for Mommy. *I was shocked and frightened because everybody knew my grandfather couldn't talk, and yet he had just talked to me! I was so thrilled and overwhelmed I didn't tell anyone that Sunday.*

The next day I was called out of class. My father told my brother and me that God had taken Grandpa to live with Him. When I got home I told my mother what grandpa had said to me the day before. She looked quizzically at me and then hugged me for a good three minutes. She whispered through her tears, "Grandpa always favored you the most."

Now I realize that my Grandfather, who hardly know me, has given me the most joyous experience I will ever have – an experience that will be ever etched in my memory.

- Beth Mazza, 18

SUMMARY OF CHAPTER FIVE   *Children are more open than adults to unusual experiences that seem other-worldly. They may have imaginary friends and live part of their lives in a make-believe world of princesses and Santa Claus. The process of growing up is, ideally, a gradual and natural transition, which, in the end, allows access to both worlds – of spirit and sense, of left and right hemispheres, of feelings and thoughts.*

In the next chapter, titled "Out of the Depths", we move from the innocence and joy of children to the anxiety and angst of those whose peak experiences save them from ruin and despair.

CHAPTER SIX

OUT OF THE DEPTHS

> While an encounter with God can happen anywhere, anytime, my research and my own life story tell me that *brokenness* is the best predictor of spiritual experience. – Barbara Bradley Hagerty

The world-famous spiritual leader and prize winning author, Eckhart Tolle, provides a fine example that PEs often come when a person has reached the emotionally lowest point possible and is contemplating suicide. Tolle tells the story in The Power of Now. "Until my thirtieth year," he writes, "I lived in a state of almost continuous anxiety interspersed with periods of suicidal depression."

One particular night, Tolle's angst reached fever pitch and he felt "a deep longing for annihilation, for nonexistence". The phrase, "I cannot live with myself any longer" kept running through his mind. Then a flash of insight made him question that strange phrase: "I cannot live with myself". Were there two of him? Perhaps only one of them was real. He contemplated this for awhile.

> Then I felt drawn into what seemed like a vortex of energy. It was a slow movement at first and then accelerated. I was gripped by an intense fear, and my body started to shake. I heard the words 'resist nothing' as if spoken inside my chest. I could feel myself being sucked into a void. It felt as if the void was inside myself rather than outside. Suddenly, there was no more fear, and I let myself fall into that void. I have no recollection of what happened next.

Eckhart Tolle had, at that time, no knowledge or experience to judge what had happened to him. He just knew that something profoundly significant had occurred and that his perception had been totally changed.

> I was awakened by the chirping of a bird outside my window. I had never heard such a sound before. My eyes were still closed, and I saw the image of a precious diamond. Yes, if a diamond could make a sound, this is what it would be like. I opened my eyes. The first light of dawn was filtering through the curtains. Without any thought, I felt, I knew, that there is infinitely more to light than we realize. That soft luminosity filtering through the curtains was love itself. Tears came into my eyes. I got up and walked around the room. I recognized the room, and yet I know that I had had never truly seen it before. Everything was fresh and pristine, as if it had just come into existence. I picked up things, a pencil, an empty bottle, marveling at the beauty and aliveness of it all. That day I

walked around the city in utter amazement at the miracle of life on earth, as If I had just been born into this world.

For the next few months, I lived in a state of uninterrupted deep peace and bliss. After that, it diminished somewhat in intensity, or perhaps it just seemed to because it became my natural state.

From a college student about the death of her cat, Siam:

Two years ago, my mother called me at work to tell me some terrible news. She had accidentally run over my Siamese cat, Siam. I was very upset for I had had my cat since I was a small child and loved her very much. I cried all that day and night. When I finally went to bed, I cried even harder because she always slept with me. I lay there and said a prayer.

All of a sudden, I heard Siam's purr. The sound seemed to be right near my ear, but in the distance at the same time. It gave me a calm and peaceful feeling.

I felt as if God was letting me spend a last minute with her, and letting me know she was alive and fine and in His hands.

I fell asleep with that purr. I will never forget that experience, and I shall always know she's happy.

- Betsy Glenn, Student

MARTIN LUTHER KING, JR

The leaders, heroes and saints of each generation were not always exemplars of strength, courage and love. Dr. Martin Luther king,

Jr. symbolized for the Civil Rights Movement a tower of strength, tenacity and heroic devotion to the ideal of non-violence.

But it was not always so. At an early point in the Montgomery, Alabama, boycott, King was scared and ready to give up. Repeated death threats against him and his family had triggered fountains of fear within him. Later to become a powerful voice for non-violence, at this time he was sleeping with a gun under his pillow. He felt his faith weakening. His worries and terror came to a climax on a Friday night, January 27, 1956, less than two months after Rosa Parks had been arrested on a Montgomery bus.

Then, on that fateful night, Martin Luther King had the most profound spiritual experience of his life. He went to his kitchen to get a cup of coffee and sat at the kitchen table. He tells of the mountain-top experience that came to him in his first book, Stride Toward Freedom.

I was ready to give up. With my cup of coffee sitting untouched before me, I tried to think of a way to move out of the picture without appearing a coward. In this state of exhaustion, when my courage had all but gone, I decided to take my problem to God. With my head in my hands, I bowed over the kitchen table and prayed aloud.

The words I spoke to God that midnight are still vivid in my memory. 'I am taking a stand for what I believe is right. But now I'm afraid. The people are looking to me for leadership, and if I stand before them without strength and courage, they too will falter. I am at the end of my powers. I have nothing left. I've come to the point where I can't face it alone.'

At that moment, I experienced the presence of the Divine as I had never experienced God before. It seemed as though I could hear the quiet assurance of an inner voice saying: "Stand up for justice, stand up for truth, and God will be at

your side forever." Almost at once my fears began to go. My uncertainty disappeared. I was ready to face anything. (Italics added) (pp. 114,115)

Note that the Friday night experience had come when King was in despair and felt at the end of his own strength. For the rest of his life King often referred to his visit to the mountain-top. His life had been changed forever. Neither dynamite, nor threats, nor fear, nor worry – nothing would stop him from his mission of deliverance. On the night before he was killed, he spoke (in eloquent night language) about this experience 12 years before: "We've got some difficult days ahead, but it doesn't matter with me now because I've been to the mountain top, and I've looked over, and I've seen the promised land. I may not get there with you, but I want you to know tonight, that we as a people will get to the promised land."

THE CREATIVE ENERGY OF SISTER PAT'S CANCER

Sister Patricia Murphy is a North Carolina Catholic nun who has recently developed an intrusive cancer which is causing significant disruption in her life. After moving out of the depths, she is able to speak to her cancer of her "weird longing" to give it love for the "many goods" this gift has brought her.

Letter to a Visiting Cancer

**Is there anyone who doesn't fear you
Doesn't want to cut out the very word and thought of you?
You've come to visit me – no advance notice
Taken up residence where I could not see you.
Until like a hermit crab you'd made my innards your home
And unpacked all your powers.**

Though you are destructive of so much life
Like a problem child or unruly animal –
I have a weird longing to give you love
The love no one wants to give you.
Yet – you must move out dear one
Find your own life.
Killing both of us leaves you homeless and feared.
Let me hold you close for a moment
Thank you for the many goods I've known because of you
But there is a door, open wide
You must find a creative energy that blesses
I send you to that place lovingly
I will take your memory as gift into my new living
Of the sweetness and incredible meaning of life
Go now – have a life
I will be more than OK.

"PEAK EXPERIENCES HELP TO PREVENT SUICIDES" - A. MASLOW

The late novelist William Styron had a lifetime struggle with depression. In his 1990 book, <u>Darkness Visible: A Memoir of Madness,</u> he speaks of the darkest time of his life when he was on the verge of self-destruction. Feeling that he could not get through another day, he was making preparations for suicide.

My wife had gone to bed, and I had forced myself to watch the tape of a movie in which a young actress, who had been in a play of mine, was cast in a small part. At one point in the film, which had been set in late nineteenth-century Boston, the characters moved down the hallway of a music conservatory, beyond the wall of which, from unseen musicians, came a contralto voice, a sudden soaring passage from the Brahms *Alto Rhapsody.*

This sound, which like all music –indeed, like all pleasure – I had been numbly unresponsive to for months, pierced my heart like a dagger, and in a flood of swift recollection I thought of all the joys the house had known: the children who had rushed through its rooms, the festivals, the love and work…. (p. 66)

The intense experience of hearing the Brahms musical passage had occasioned a peak experience, a mountain-top moment that brought Styron a clarity of knowing that cut through his morass of melancholy. …The next day he admitted himself into a psychiatric hospital.

———

When deaths occur, peak experiences abound. Thousands of cases have been reported testifying to the appearance of the dying one, who is either seen physically or whose presence is unmistakably felt at the very moment of death. A woman in her seventies tells the following incident about the death of her grandfather and how it affected her mother, Ruth.

My grandfather, Ruth's father, and my mother, Ruth, were very close. He was a man of few words. Although his education ended with the eighth grade, he loved to learn; he taught himself trigonometry 'for the fun of it'. He could relate to machines more easily than to people. He had designed his own house, invented various machines, and endlessly tinkered with clocks. When her dad wasn't tinkering, he liked exploring nature and often took Ruth with him. Ruth learned about plants, geology and gained an appreciation for the outdoors as she accompanied him hiking the bluffs surrounding the beautiful Wisconsin lake where they summered at their cottage. Quietly companionable, they spoke little.

The years went by, Ruth married, had children and her parents aged. Ruth could never remember her father directly telling her that he loved her. Then one day, in his nineties, her father had a stroke. She called the rescue squad and followed him to the hospital. Finally, when there seemed nothing more for her to do there, she went home to rest. She was standing in her kitchen when suddenly she felt herself immersed in the warmth of a presence. She related, "The room was filled with light and everything seemed to stand still in that perfect moment. I felt embraced in peace, joy and love. Then I heard my father's voice saying, 'I love you, Ruthie'. Those words she had longed for but had never heard rang through her very soul.

The telephone rang. It was the hospital calling to tell her that her father had died. ... She shared this with me when she was almost 90.

- Anonymous Daughter

CALLED TO BE A MESSENGER OF DEATH

Some peak experiences are quite stunning, both in themselves and in their implications. This one occurred about fifteen years ago to a woman in the Midwest.

The experience happened at the outdoor wedding reception of a dear friend. My friend seemed truly happy to have found the love of her life so the energy was light and joyful. I was excited about going to the wedding as it was being held in a beautiful place with nice music and delicious food. ...Little did I know that my understanding of life was about to radically change.

After the ceremony, I met an older, married couple, out-of-town friends of the bride. I stopped to admire their PRE-VERBAL, nine month old baby who was in his dad's arms. I remember that the first thought in my mind was "Wow! What an OLD baby" A bald head and very quiet demeanor. My next thought was "Oh, what gorgeous eyes!" As I stood there talking with the dad I found myself mesmerized by the baby's eyes, unable to take my eyes off his. As the dad shifted the weight of the baby from side to side in his arms, the baby made automatic adjustments to stay intently focused on my eyes, to the point that the father commented, "He's really focused on you, isn't he?" For my part, I was unable to look away and experienced a concentration, a flow, similar to the beams of sunlight through trees.

Through that focus, these words were transmitted to my brain (I don't know how else to describe it): "I would like you to give a message to my parents for me. I will not be here much longer. My work here is done. When the time comes, I want you to tell my parents that they were wonderful, loving parents and they could have done NOTHING to stop my death from happening. I know they will be hurting, and they are so loving that I want them to know that I love them very much."

One moment I was just a human being, going about the everyday activities of a regular human being on this planet, not really knowing about "what else was out there", and the next moment, I had proof that we are not alone on this journey called human life!

I was so exhausted and so agitated by the experience that I left the reception soon after that. What was I supposed to do with this information that came to me so clearly as though I had read the words in a book? As soon as my friend, the bride, returned from the honeymoon, I shared the experience with her and asked her advice. (The parents of the amazing baby were her friends of long standing.) We both agreed that I could not go to them and tell them that their son would die in the near future. So, I held the information in my heart.

A couple of years later, the child died in a swimming pool drowning. I wrote the parents a letter telling them of my interaction with their son and giving them his message. They were so devastated that they could not take in the information and put the letter in a desk drawer. Years later when the mother was cleaning out the drawer and found the letter, she visited me and asked me to share the wedding day experience with her. It was still as real as the day I was given the message, and the honor of being asked to be a messenger was just as awesome.

- Fran Westin

BYRON KATIE'S DISCOVERY OF "THE WORK"

> Byron Katie is one of the truly great and inspiring teachers of our time. She has been enormously helpful to me personally. I love this very wise woman.
>
> –Dr. Wayne W. Dyer
>
> A spiritual innovator for the new millennium. – Time Magazine

Byron Katie is a speaker and author who teaches a method of self-inquiry known as "The Work of Byron Katie" or simply as "The Work". Not aligned with any particular religion or tradition, she is married to the writer and translator Stephen Mitchell. "The Work" basically consists of asking ourselves four questions about a disturbing thought.

Katie says that these questions and the entire concept of "The Work" were given to her, intact and complete, on a February morning in 1986 as part of a profound, mind-shattering, revelatory peak experience. At age 43, after suffering for over ten years from deep depression, (now diagnosed as suicidal depression,) she was sleeping on the floor of a half-way house for women with eating disorders. Weighing over 200 pounds, she describes herself as a victim of frequent violent rage attacks. She had spiraled down into paranoia, rage, self-loathing, and constant thoughts of suicide; for the past two years she had not been able to leave her bedroom. She awoke with a start and with a complete and intense understanding of her situation and of the way out of it. She knew she was not only healed, but had been given a profound gift to teach others to heal.

I discovered that when I believed my thoughts, I suffered, but when I didn't believe them, I didn't suffer, and that this is true for every human being. Freedom is as simple as that. I found that suffering is optional. I found a joy within me that has never disappeared, not for a single moment.

(Byron Katie - Wikipedia)

Since 1986, Katie has introduced The Work to millions of people throughout the world via best selling books, personal appearances and through her School for The Work.

> The composer Elgar said of a young singer who was techni-
> cally perfect but lacking in feeling and expression, "She will be
> great when something breaks her heart."

WHEN GOD LAUGHED – LIGHTNING ON THE LAKE

This personal experience of "God laughing" was reported to the
writer by a 75 year old woman (since deceased) who had a summer cottage near Buffalo, New York. She also, at that time, had a
male friend and companion who was causing her grief. Excerpts
are taken from a long essay that she submitted for this book.

**God's laughter is an individual, personal experience, re-
vealed to very few.**

**It was several years ago during a deeply painful involve-
ment in life's complexities, when I felt so torn, so pulled
apart, so frustrated. I had so much love to share, so much
love and joy. Yet there was one man who would not or could
not accept that truth. His jealousy, bitterness and limitations kept him and me in a constant state of agitation, ac-
cusation and turmoil.**

**My very soul cried out: Escape, escape; get away from
that complaining voice. Find silence, find peace, my heart
cried...Then came the wonder-filled climax. I walked on the
lonely beach near the cottage. I was in despair. It was sunset on a warm breezy summer evening. Claps of thunder
rumbled in the distance, coming ever closer. Wind clouds
gathered over Lake Erie. Warm waves, white and red,
lapped the sandy shore.**

Then, as if drawn into Nature herself, I waded out into the water. Lightening flashed overhead. I didn't care that my clothing hung wet or that my hair felt cool as the rain began to fall. I loved the wind, the waves the power of the thunder. It filled me with a sense of peace, so tired was I of the battles and the noise of angry voices. I thought, 'How easy it would be to keep on walking deeper and deeper – to drown and be finished with it all. So easy!

Hypnotized, waist deep, I swayed from side to side like a baby in its mother's arms. Lightning zigzagged all round. Rain like a baptism drenched my face, forming jumping bubbles in the gleaming water.

Then, miracle of miracle – a rainbow. "My God, " I cried, "How great thou art!" Suddenly came the unmistakable sound of mighty laughter. The voice was so clear, so compassionate. Powerful and sure came the words:

"OH, THOSE LITTLE MEN!"

I laughed and laughed and God laughed with me. How we enjoyed each other! Ecstasy! Time meant nothing. My whole being responded with a current of electricity which was pure Joy. ...

If I live to be a thousand years old, I'll still draw upon that personal experience when my God became a living, loving, laughing God.

-Sylvia Kathleen Smith

Kat McQuown is an artist and writer presently living in North Carolina. The major healing story she tells here combines several of our arbitrary categories; the beauty of nature, magical sacred places and a broken heart combine in this recollection of a life-changing peak experience.

I was a few months away from my 50th birthday and had just escaped from a very physically and emotionally abusive relationship. A friend in Nevada City, California, needed someone to caretake her property and pets for a few weeks, and it offered me a refuge to heal and to plan for a future. The home was beautiful – set on several acres surrounded by a wonderful forest of pines and oaks.

I spent many days weeping and worrying, reading, writing in my journals, then weeping some more. I took walks in the forest daily. It was the only time I felt peaceful and calm. On the third day I happened upon a truly beautiful scene – a large moss covered boulder which overlooked a small, but noisy, creek. Two tall pine trees stood 20 feet apart on either side of the boulder like protective sentinels. Large oaks and birches offered plenty of cool shade. Sunlight filtered through the trees and danced like sparkling jewels on the small creek. It felt magical and sacred, and I felt safe and calm. I would often meditate and pray there – for healing and guidance. Often I stayed for hours.

The final day of my stay arrived; my friend was coming home the next day. There was an unusual deep fog that morning, but by 11am it had lifted and I took off for my last walk alone in the forest. ...I wanted to remember everything about this place so I took my time seeing and hearing and breathing in the magic of nature.

Edward M. O'Keefe Ph.D.

When I arrived at the boulder, I kicked off my shoes and stood on the beautiful soft moss wiggling my toes into it. I looked up at the canopy of trees overhead and stretched out my arms towards those large magnificent pines and took a deep breath and slowly closed my eyes; it was totally silent and a deep feeling of intense gratitude welled up inside of me. I felt both peaceful and joyful.

At that moment everything changed. Energy seemed to be coming up through my feet and legs and right out the top of my head. I could feel energy running through my arms It was the most amazing feeling I had ever had. I felt as light as a feather. I couldn't even feel my body anymore. I opened my eyes slowly, not wanting to do anything to stop this incredible feeling. I looked at my arms and they were really not visible. All I saw was shimmering light going from one pine tree to the other –THROUGH ME! I could no longer feel the earth under me. A feeling of pure joy and intense love filled me up and I felt like I was connected to the whole universe. The intensity of the feeling heightened. I felt like I was just going to disappear and I was a bit frightened at that. At that point the feeling ended abruptly. ...I stayed for quite sometime trying to recreate it and finally, several hours later, returned to the house.

There have been many ups and downs since that day. I moved to Europe for a bit, then across this country to North Carolina where my small house burned to the ground. I built another beautiful home. I've had cancer and knee surgery and a few short-lived romances. I have mostly wonderful days and I am so grateful for all of it. I still spend a lot of time in the forest which surrounds my new home and I am ever hopeful I can experience that divine bliss again. I am forever grateful to have had such a gift even once. As a result of it, *I now have no fear of death. I imagine that when we die, we become this blissful shimmering energy bringing light to the world.*

———————

SUMMARY OF CHAPTER 6   *Poet Gerard Manley Hopkins expressed it this way in his famous poem, "The Hound of Heaven". He has the sufferer, representing the human condition, complain to God:*

**Ah! must-
Designer Infinite!-
Ah! must Thou char the wood ere Thou can'st limn* with it?**

Must we be broken by life's sorrows and difficulties before we can reach wisdom, before we can be raised up to mountain-top heights? It appears that, for some individuals, though certainly not all, peak experiences come only when personal suffering is at its worst. Perhaps some light will be shed on this anomaly in the next chapter when we discuss barriers to PEs.

*limn – draw or paint

CHAPTER SEVEN

WHAT'S HOLDING US BACK - RESISTANCE FORCES

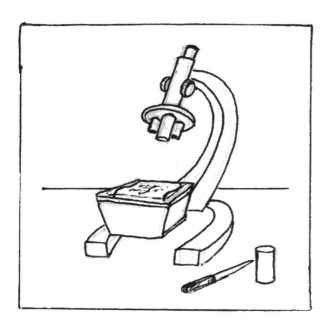

POGO AND KURT LEWIN

In one of the memorable moments of cartoonist Walt Kelly's long-running comic strip (1949-1975), Pogo, the wry and articulate swamp possum, announces "We have met the enemy and he is us". It is a truism that we do not have to look outside of ourselves for resistance to our own better impulses and intentions.

Similarly, within any situation, personal or social, observed social psychologist Kurt Lewin (1890 – 1947), there are both *driving forces* facilitating movement toward a goal and *resistance forces* hindering movement toward that goal.

Lewin is recognized as the founder of social psychology and was one of the first to study group dynamics and organizational development. He also laid the foundations for what is now known as sensitivity training. The concepts of opposing forces, some driving towards a goal and others resisting movement away from the status quo, was Lewin's basic framework for what is called Force Field Analysis. "This principle is a significant contribution to the fields of social science, psychology, organizational development, process management, and change management". (Wikepedia: Kurt Lewin)

Based on the work of Abraham Maslow and many other authors, scholars and spiritual leaders, *the goal of peak experiences seems to be the growth of the individual experiencing the transcendent moment and the enhancement of the entire race of mankind.* The use of Lewin's framework helps us conceptualize the elements in the change process: on the one hand, the driving forces leading us to personal and collective growth, and, on the other hand, the resistance forces tending to block change and growth.

To effect positive change, according to Lewin, one can either *increase the driving forces* or *decrease the resistance forces.* We believe this distinction is most helpful in approaching the present subject of peak experiences and human growth. It is our contention that the driving forces toward positive change and growth are innate and already fully available (though most often not recognized, acknowledged or used) within the human psyche. We believe with Robert Browning who speaks to us in the night language of metaphor:

IMPRISONED SPLENDOR

Truth is within ourselves; it takes no rise
From outward things, what'er you may believe.
There is an inmost center in us all,
Where truth abides in fullness; and around,
Wall upon wall, the gross flesh hems us in,
This perfect, clear perception – which is truth.
A baffling and perverting carnal mesh
Binds it, and makes all error: and to know
Rather consists in opening a way
Whence the imprisoned splendor may escape,
Than in effecting entry for a light
Supposed to be without.

From "Paracelsus"

Peak experiences can be viewed as royal avenues to our progressive recognition of the splendor within us as individuals and, far more significantly, within the identity of the collective human. Most important to our process, then, is for us to find ways to allow the inner splendor to come forth. The primary means to achieve this goal is to delete, or at least minimize, the resistance forces that stand in the path of change.

Human history has created many resistance forces to our recognition of ourselves as potential spiritual giants. They are rampant within our society. Barbara Ehrenreich in her masterful 2007 work, Dancing in the Streets: A History of Collective Joy, identifies a whole host of formidable forces arrayed against people's achieving the farther reaches of their potential, including the focus of her work, communal joy and bonding. She examines many obstacles, including organized religion, the Reformation, especially Puritanism, militarism, imperialism, fascism, and capitalism, with special attention to the continuing Industrial Revolution.

Ehrenreich skillfully traces through history "the techniques of ecstasy" developed by humans to both encourage and express communal joy and bonding. This behavior, so rare and unwelcome now in our modern societies that we term it 'savage', 'primitive', and 'animalistic', has been systematically and most often cruelly, suppressed. As this suppression became almost universal, personal depression, for the first time in history, became a huge problem, now the fourth largest cause of death and disability in the world. Ehrenreich devotes an entire chapter, titled "An Epidemic of Melancholy", to this highly significant negative result of the suppression of natural outlets of communal excitement and joy.

From Ehrenreich's list and from our own observations, we have chosen to consider four of the forces resistant to the occurrence and nurturing of peak experiences:

> A. The 'Rotten-to-the-core'/original sin dogma.
> B. The Jonah Complex – fear of our greatness.
> C. Automatic, robotic behavior – which keeps us unaware.
> D. The fear of ridicule from the scientific community.

We feel that these four influences are very significant in the lives and psyches of many people <u>and</u> that attention to them has the potential to effect positive changes in readers' attitudes and receptivity. While we may feel virtually powerless to counter world-wide militarism, for example, we can take personal steps to combat these four resistance forces and thereby remove impediments to our ability to change.

A - ROTTEN-TO-THE-CORE/ORIGINAL SIN DOGMA

The first and most important of the Resistance Forces we wish to highlight is what Martin Seligman calls "the rotten-to-the-core dogma", a pervasive view of human nature which recurs across many cultures".

Seligman, the founder of the Positive Psychology Movement and a past president of the American Psychological Association (as was Abraham Maslow before him), says, in his 1992 book, <u>Authentic Happiness,</u> that while the religious concept of original sin, arising from traditional Western Christianity, is the oldest manifestation of such doctrinal thinking, 'the rotten-to-the-core' influence goes far beyond those roots and pervades our entire society. He blames particularly Sigmund Freud for this.

Freud dragged this doctrine into the twentieth century psychology, defining all of civilization (including modern morality, science, religion, and technological progress) as just an elaborate defense against basic conflicts over infantile sexuality and aggression...Freud's philosophy... finds its way into daily psychological and psychiatric practice, wherein patients scour their past for the negative impulses and events that have formed their identities. Thus the competitiveness of Bill Gates is really his desire to outdo his father, and Princess Diana's opposition to land mines was merely the outcome of sublimating her murderous hatred for Prince Charles and the other royals. (Introduction, page x)

Seligman also cites past and current understandings of human nature in the arts and sciences for exhibiting time and time again this negative view of humans. He concludes, "I cannot say this too strongly: In spite of the widespread acceptance of the rotten-to-the-core dogma in the religious and secular world, there is not one shred of evidence that strength and virtue are derived from negative motivation". (p. xi)

As for our topic, it is clear that if people consider themselves seriously blighted by the very fact of being born into a cursed race, peak experiences will probably not be recognized, welcomed or nurtured. Because most PE's, by definition, are transcendent and often ecstatic in nature and hence close to religious and spiritual experiences, it behooves us to consider more closely the so-called Fall of Man and the beginnings of the Original Sin mythology.

> Jan Frazier is the author of the profound and beautifully written <u>When Fear Falls Away</u> . She writes of the earlier effects – prior to her mountain-top experiences - of any feelings of unworthiness:
>
> "I now see ego as everything that once interfered with my awareness of the deeper reality – including any ideas of relative worthiness. The belief in my own unworthiness for liberation was part of what was in the way, part of what kept my ego substantial, real-seeming. ...Contrary to what I believed, it isn't the 'humble' self that becomes liberated. It's when all the definitions of self fall apart that enlightened consciousness can finally be experienced." (pp. 101,102)

ORIGINAL SIN

Enid Hoffman is a practitioner and teacher of Huna, an ancient way of life and philosophy that comes from Hawaii via the Polynesian Islands. In her book, <u>Huna: A Beginner's Guide,</u> she eloquently considers how our psyches are formed as children.

> **From early childhood on, we are programmed to accept a set of values already established by others – what is right and what is wrong, what is good or bad ...(Later) we forget their origin, and we become convinced that they are our own values...**
>
> **In our early religious instruction many of us have heard an unforgettable story of our beginnings as human beings. The story relates that man and woman were created as perfect beings without fear, anger, or guilt. 'Original sin' is a**

part of that story that illustrates disobedience to authority. By disobeying the one in authority, this original man and woman first experienced guilt and shame. We have carried this potential for feeling guilt and shame within our very bones from the time we first heard that story...

It hides in our subconscious like a slow-moving poison, inhibiting us and creating a context wherein it is better to hide what we feel, hold back our natural impulses and suppress expression. Doing what we want becomes a sinful act if it is in contradiction to what others wish. (pp. 28,29)

Hoffman goes on to say that in Huna there is only one sin and that sin is personal and not communal – to knowingly hurt another person. That is a far cry from the Christian West's focus on our having a sinful nature and an impulse toward multiple catalogues of transgressions.

Matthew Fox, formerly a Roman Catholic priest-theologian of the Dominican religious order, is now a priest ordained in the Anglican tradition. He was forced out (excommunicated) by the Catholic Church for his writings, considered heretical, about this very doctrine of Original Sin. Fox, a prolific author, is the founder of, and lead spokesperson for, the movement called Creation Spirituality. Fox published a great deal about mystical and peak experiences, and wrote of the all-pervasiveness of the effects of what he calls, "the famous doctrine of original sin":

There is no question in my mind that among those who call themselves Christian, whether practicing or not, ninety-nine percent know about original sin, and barely one percent have ever in their lives heard about original blessing. This is the great price we have paid in the West for following a one-sided fall/redemption theology....Fall/redemption theology has ignored the blessing that creation is because of its anthropomorphic preoccupation with

sin! The result has been, among other things, the loss of pleasure from spirituality and, with this loss, the increase of pain, of injustice, of sado-masochism, and of distrust. Nineteen billion years before there was any sin on earth, there was blessing.

While a review of Biblical scholarship about this issue would be instructive, it would take us too far afield from our purposes in this book. We present here only a very brief outline of the conclusions of reputable scholars and researchers about the historical origins of the original sin doctrine.

1. The Garden of Eden story recounted in the Book of Genesis is reputedly the basis for the doctrine that all men (and women) inherit the sin of Adam (and Eve). However, this understanding was never part of the Jewish Scriptural tradition, much more ancient than the Christian era, nor was it ever the view of Christian (Eastern) Orthodoxy.

2. Augustine, fifth century Bishop of Hippo in North Africa, deemed one of the greatest teachers of western Christianity by author/scholar/historian Elaine Pagels, single-handedly created the concept of original sin. He used his own understandings of the "Fall of Man" Eden story from Genesis and of a passage from the Epistle to the Romans (Romans 5:12).

According to Pagels, Augustine "effectively transformed much of the teaching of the Christian faith. (His) theory of human depravity – and, correspondingly, the political means to control it – replaced the previous ideology of human freedom. ... Astonishingly, Augustine's radical views prevailed, eclipsing for future generations of Western Christians the consensus of three centuries of Christian tradition."

Pagels goes on to exhaustively detail Augustine's doctrine of original sin, of great importance to our study because "ever since Augustine, the hereditary transmission of original sin had been the official doctrine of the Catholic Church." (p. 134).

She ends her masterful study, <u>Adam, Eve, and</u> <u>the Serpent</u>, in these words, "From the fifth century on, Augustine's pessimistic views of sexuality, politics, and human nature would become the dominant influence on western Christianity, both Catholic and Protestant, and color all western culture, Christian or not, ever since".

Born in grief and fear, this doctrine (Original Sin) has left Western Christianity with a difficult legacy that linked sexuality with sin and helped to alienate men and women from their humanity. - <u>The Case For God</u>, Karen Armstrong, p. 122

For those who wish further study of these matters, besides Matthew Fox's <u>Original Blessing</u> and Pagel's book, we highly recommend Richard Heinberg's <u>Memories and Visions of Paradise: Exploring the Universal Myth of a Lost Golden Age.</u>

In conclusion, we judge Augustine's Original Sin doctrine and its subsequent expansion into the 'rotten-to-the-core' dogma, considered together, as the most serious barrier, or Resistant Force, to the appreciation and spread of peak experiences. Such negative teachings have, in the Western world, seriously affected the self image of millions.

B- THE JONAH COMPLEX: FEAR OF OUR ABILITIES AND POSSIBILITIES

Our deepest fear is not that we are inadequate; our deepest fear is that we are powerful beyond measure.

- Nelson Mandella

> Human beings do not realize the extent to which their own
> sense of defeat prevents them from doing things they could
> do perfectly well. The peak experience induces the recognition
> that your own powers are far greater than you imagined them
>
> - Colin Wilson

Clearly allied to 'rotten-to-the-core' dogma, a second Resistance Force to the appreciation and fostering of PE's and other manifestations of the higher levels of human aspiration is what Maslow termed the Jonah Complex. Maslow described the complex as "(T)he evasion of one's own growth, the setting of low levels of aspiration, the fear of doing what one is capable of doing, voluntary self-crippling, pseudo-stupidity, mock humility."

Old Testament Jonah, an eighth century BCE prophet, was ordered by God to preach and prophesy against the wickedness of the inhabitants of the city of Nineveh. Reluctant to undertake this onerous duty, Jonah goes instead to Jaffa and embarks as a passenger on a sailing ship in the other direction. The ship nearly sinks in a storm; the guilty Jonah, after being thrown overboard, is swallowed by a whale, and the ship is saved. Jonah, still miraculously alive after three days, escapes the whale and, sheepishly and still unwillingly, fulfills his call to Nineveh.

A peak experience may sometimes be considered a sacred call, the personal promptings of evolution, and, while gratifying to our sense of self at some level, it may be massively frightening at other levels of our egos. In his 1997 book, <u>Callings: Finding and Following an Authentic Life,</u> Gregg Levoy reminds us that even Moses, on being called to free the Israelites from Egypt, argued with God that he was not capable, that he was a stutterer, etc. Levoy goes on,

**We all have a part of us, forever incalculable and arch, that
simply fears change and reacts to it with a reflective flinch,**

the way snails recoil at the touch, or birds bolt for the sky. And a calling is a messenger of change...

Resistance is not only universal, but also instinctive. It may be contrary to the open-mindedness and resilience we would prefer and that seems so necessary to getting through life with a measure of grace, but it's still involuntary. Out brains are wired for it...If we had no impulse toward caution, our curiosities would probably kill us. We'd probably step out of the car at the safari park. (p. 18)

We fear our highest possibilities. We are generally afraid to become that which we can glimpse in our most perfect moments, under conditions of great courage. We enjoy and even thrill to the godlike possibilities we see in ourselves in such peak moments. And yet, we simultaneously shiver with weakness, awe, and fear before these very same possibilities.
- Abraham Maslow (quoted in Hoffman, The Right to Be Human – p. 217

O God! It is a fearful thing to see the human soul take wing.
- Lord Byron

SAMPLE ANTIDOTE PE

Fear of various kinds keeps many of us from achieving our potential. Most PEs are antidotes to all manner of fears, including the fear of success. Student David Krieger tells of over-coming performance anxiety when he was in his twenties.

Our band was going to play for the first time in front of an audience. We were all scared and kept saying to each other that we'd never be able to pull it off. More and more people were showing up at the party, many from our school. The

thought of facing them all after making a fool of myself horrified me. When we were getting changed, I began to shake – literally. I even spilled my beer. When we walked out for the opening song, I looked at their smiling faces, slightly tinted by the bright lights. They looked like hungry wolves, ready to devour the fallen lambs.

But when the drum started its beat, something about me changed. I lost my fear completely. And I knew, somehow I knew, that the other band members were feeling the same way, too, full of confidence and ready to go. We not only did the whole gig without mistakes, we even had fun.

After the gig, people came up to talk to us. I stood there looking at my amp, and feeling like the center of the world. I got a feeling then that I only get from playing. That feeling is the high point of my life!

C – THE ROBOT: THE AUTOMATIC PILOT

Another in what we have called the personal Resistance Forces that keep us from peak experiences is what Colin Wilson calls "The Robot", the automatic pilot in our subconscious who is always waiting to take over and run things for us, lest we stay awake and alert. Wilson, perhaps the foremost student of the peak experience phenomenon since Abraham Maslow, considers the theory of the robot one of his central ideas to which he often returns in his voluminous writings. The following excerpt is from one of his many books, New Pathways in Psychology: Maslow and the Post-Freudian Revolution.

When I learned to type, I had to do it painfully and with much nervous wear and tear. But at a certain stage, a miracle occurred, and this complicated operation was 'learned' by a useful robot whom I conceal in my subconscious mind.

Now I only have to think about what I want to say: my robot secretary does the typing. He is really very useful. He also drives the car for me...

He has one enormous disadvantage. If I discover a new symphony that moves me deeply, or a poem or a painting, this bloody robot promptly insists on getting in on the act. And when I listen to the symphony for the third time, he begins to anticipate every note. He begins to listen to it automatically, and I lose all the pleasure. He is most annoying when I am tired, because then he tends to take over most of my functions without even asking me. I have even caught him making love to my wife...

Heaven lies about us in our infancy, as Wordsworth pointed out, because the robot hasn't taken over yet. (p. 20)

Wilson points out that the robot is necessary for our survival. Without his services, we would be overwhelmed with details and unable to function in the world. "But he also acts as a filter that cuts out the freshness, the newness, of everyday life...In developing the robot, we have solved one enormous problem – and created another". (p. 21)

Colin Wilson believes that we need peak experiences from time to time to rescue ourselves from our essential laziness. For the robot, in its very efficiency, tends to diminish life and the enjoyment of life. A significant purpose in much of Wilson's prolific literary efforts is to share insights he has developed about how to get our lives back from this faithful automatic servant we have created. Unless we are consciously careful, our automatic pilots will rob us of our joy and purpose in life.

Are you a god?, they asked the Buddha. "No," he replied.
Are you an angel then?   "No."
A saint?   "No."
Then what are you?   Replied the Buddha, "I am awake."

D – FEAR OF RIDICULE FROM THE SCIENTIFIC COMMU-NITY

It used to be that the scientific community leaned heavily towards disdaining, sometimes openly and always at least subtly, the 'spiritual' – those aspects of life that could not be weighed, measured or neatly catalogued. People who spoke of other-worldly, religious or transcendent experiences were considered deluded or delusional, perhaps psychotic or, at least, neurotic. We must remember that modern science was painfully born in the late Medieval period when organized religious narrowness and superstition did its best to constrain what we now call modern scientific thought. Later, gaining ascendency and societal acceptance, rational, materialistic, often atheistic, science was seen as an enemy of anything that seemed spiritual, transcendent and 'mystical'.

It is hardly surprising, then, with this kind of hostile environment, that 'peakers'- those having transcendent, mountain-top experiences – would be very reluctant to expose themselves to criticism and ridicule from a community which puts its faith in 'scientific values.' And scientists, researchers, physicians, etc. are often seen as people of great and grave authority, the gurus and priests of the new scientific world.

> "...scientists today often occupy a social role like that of 'high priests in earlier cultures, telling laypeople and each other what is and isn't 'real', and, consequently, what is or isn't valuable and sane. Unfortunately, the dominant materialistic and reductionist psychosocial climate of contemporary science, scientism, rejects and suppresses both having and sharing transcendent, transpersonal, and altered-state experiences.   – Charles Tart, p. 366

The above quote is taken from the latest book of Charles Tart, Ph.D., an internationally known author and scientist whose work includes more than 50 years of research on the nature of consciousness, altered states and parapsychology. He is one of the founders of the field of Transpersonal Psychology. The 2009 book is titled <u>The End of Materialism: How Evidence of the Paranormal Is Bringing Science and Spirit Together.</u>

Tart abhors what he calls this 'a priori' culture of exclusionism. He calls it "scientism" to reject out of hand the transpersonal world for which there is so much evidence collected over many years. His 50 plus year career was spent studying the transpersonal, subjecting such experiences to rigorous scientific standards. Dr. Larry Dossey calls Tart a "legendary psychologist and psi researcher... who helped invent the new image of consciousness through five decades of meticulous research. Tart's inspiring, majestic image of consciousness will prevail because of two compelling reasons: it is built on good science and it more fully accounts for who we humans are and how we behave." (Book endorsement)

Charles Tart is working to change the attitude of the scientific community. And many other well-known scholars and scientists are working towards the same end. In their excellent book, <u>Why God Won't Go Away</u>. medical researchers, Andrew Newberg, M.D. and the late Eugene D'Aquille, M.D., Ph.D., summarize modern scientific studies and their own work which clearly indicates that the religious impulse, the search for meaning and transcendence, is rooted in the biology of the brain. The emerging field of 'neurotheology' shows that human beings are wired for transcendence.

A few quotes from the book follow.

In the midst of this scientific revelation (Lyell's work in geology and Darwin's in evolution) Nietzsche proclaimed God dead. It's important, however, to realize that the God he thought science had killed, the God that was no longer compatible with rational thinking, was the personal Creator God of the Bible. *There is nothing that we have found in science or reason to refute the concept of a higher mystical reality.* (p. 169)

At the heart of our theory is a neurological model that provides a link between mystical experiences and observable brain function. *In simplest terms, the brain seems to have the built-in ability to transcend the perception of an individual self. We have theorized that this talent of self-transcendence lies at the root of the religious urge. (p.174)*

This is ... the goal of the emerging field of neurotheology, to understand the link between brain function and all important aspects of religion. (p. 175)

Although students of the spiritual might object to the emphasis on the material brain as central to these researchers' argument – with the implied identification of mind with brain - nevertheless, these new developments and especially the new and more open mindset of well-known scientists, bode well for the future.

However strong the prejudice against the spiritual in the scientific community may have been in the past, today that attitude is changing. The Age of Galileo is long over. Since Einstein and the rise of modern physics, especially quantum physics, it's a new exciting world open to awe, amazement, the scientific method AND spiritual insight.

———

CASE STUDY – DR. BRUCE LIPTON, CELL BIOLOGY SCIENTIST

We end, for now, our detour into the supposed science/spiritual dichotomy by considering the current case of a leading cell researcher, Bruce Lipton, Ph.D., who exemplifies a 'crossover pioneer' between the two realms. We relate some of the PEs of Dr. Lipton for three reasons. Not only is he currently acting as a bridge between the scientific and spiritual worlds through his writings, he is also a fine example of 'guidance peak experiences' which have progressively led him to choose and further his career in science research. Thirdly, it was his most profound PE that gave him the insight and understanding to cement his own paradigm shift about the nature of cellular biology, thereby becoming the spokesperson (or the whipping boy for those scientific traditionalists) for a new way to view the human cell and a new way to view our whole reality.

We will consider how Lipton's journey through life has been guided by periodic PEs. The following material is taken from his 2005 paradigm-smashing book, The Biology of Belief: Unleashing the Power of Consciousness, Matter, and Miracles. We start with an event when Bruce was seven years old.

I was seven years old when I stepped up onto a small box in Mrs. Novak's second grade classroom, high enough to plop my eye right onto the lens and eyepiece of a microscope. Alas, I was too close to see anything but a blob of light. Finally, I calmed down enough to listen to instructions to back off from the eyepiece. *And then it happened, an event so dramatic that it would set the course of the rest of my life.* A paramecium swam into the field. *I was mesmerized. ...My whole being was transfixed* by the alien world of this cell that for me was more exciting than today's computer-animated special effects movies....

Immediately after school, I ran home and excitedly relayed my microscopic adventure to my mother. Using my best second-grade powers of persuasion, I asked, then begged, then cajoled my mother into getting me a microscope, where I could spend hours mesmerized by this alien world that I could access via the miracle of optics. (p. 19)

Later, in graduate school, Lipton is finally allowed to use an electron microscope which magnifies the cells to 100,000 times their size. He is again overwhelmed.

My awe at being at the edge of this scientific frontier was palpable....Most of the rush I experienced came from my vision of myself as a pioneer, traversing territory that had never been seen by human eyes. ...it was the electron microscope that brought me face to face with the molecules that were the very foundation of life itself. I knew that buried within the cytoarchitecture of the cell were clues that would provide insight into the mysteries of life....

I saw my future. I knew I was going to be e cellular biologist whose research would focus on scrutinizing every nuance of the cell's ultrastructure to gain insights into the secrets of cellular life. ...My exploration of the 'secrets of life' led me into a research career studying the character of cloned human cells grown in tissue culture. (p. 21)

DIFFICULT TIMES – OUT OF THE DEPTHS

At this time, Lipton relates, he didn't believe in God. "I was, after all, a traditional biologist for whom God's existence is an unnecessary question: life is the consequence of blind chance, the flip of a friendly card or, to be more precise, the random shake of genetic dice". And things were not going well. "I thought I was one of those people victimized by a missing or mutant happiness gene." His father has just died after a long emotionally-difficult illness, he was very busy at work, and was in the middle of an emotionally and economically draining divorce. "I was economically challenged and homeless", he says.

Finally, he snapped. When he received a call from a banker that his mortgage application would not be honored, Bruce threw the phone through the glass door of his office at the Anatomy Department at the University of Wisconsin where he was an assistant professor, all the while screaming, "Get me out of here!". A short-term sabbatical at a medical school in the Caribbean followed, which gave Bruce a new lease on life. He returned happier, but even more radicalized. "(I was now) a screaming radical bent on challenging the sacred foundational beliefs of biology. I even began to openly criticize Charles Darwin and the wisdom of his theory of evolution. In the eyes of most other biologists, my behavior was tantamount to a priest bursting into the Vatican and claiming the Pope was a fraud." (p. 25)

Feeling that perhaps the academic life was not for him, Lipton gave up his tenured position and went on a tour with a rock band; he even produced a laser show with Yanni while on the road. Soon, however, "I wound down my midlife crisis," gave up the music business and returned to the Caribbean to teach cell biology again.

The stage was now set for the prime eureka moment of Bruce Lipton's life. It happened more than twenty-five years ago.

In 1985, I was living in a rented house in the spice-drenched Caribbean island of Grenada teaching at yet another 'offshore' medical school. It was 2 A.M. and I was up revisiting years of notes on the biology , chemistry and physics of the cell membrane. At the time I was reviewing the mechanics of the membrane, trying to get a grasp of how it worked as an information processing system. *That is when I experienced a moment of insight that transformed me…* into a membrane-centered biologist who no longer had any excuses for messing up his life. (p. 89)

Lipton goes into the details of his mental reworking the definition of the membrane – "a liquid crystal semiconductor with gates and channels". Then he realizes that the phrases are very familiar. He had just read a description of a computer chip for a new computer he had bought, "a crystal semiconductor with gates and channels." This serendipitous merging led to a moment of great insight that staggered the imagination of Lipton as he began to consider the implications of this "discovery".

I was momentarily stunned when I realized that the identical nature of their definitions was not a coincidence. The cell membrane was indeed a structural and functional equivalent (homologue) of a silicon chip!

...(This means) that it is both appropriate and instructive to better fathom the workings of the cell by comparing it to a personal computer. (p. 92)

Laypeople may not see much to emote about in the above insight, but to a cell scientist like Bruce Lipton, it was staggering in its implications. (Twelve years later, it was scientifically confirmed by an Australian research consortium.) The insight means, according to Lipton,

that *both computers and cells are programmable... and that the programmer lies outside the computer/cell.* Biological behavior and gene activity are dynamically linked to information from the environment, which is downloaded into the cell.

I realized in those early morning hours that even though biological thought is still preoccupied with genetic determinism, leading edge cell research, which continues to unfold the mystery of the Magical Membrane in ever more complex detail, tells a far different story.

While much of the scientific community was focused in recent years on the much hyped Genome Project, cataloguing the various genes in our DNA, Lipton was engaged in considering the many implications of his astounding peak experience of discovery, not only its scientific implications, but the life-changing personal upheavals that it produced. These very clearly mixed together in Lipton's heart and mind. Excerpts follow describing the profound implications of this insight.

- That Caribbean moment not only transformed me into a membrane-centered biologist, it also transformed me from an agnostic scientist into a card-carrying mystic who believes that eternal life transcends the body. (94)

- I saw something in it (the experience) that was so profound, it immediately transformed my life. In the first instant of my big 'aha', my brain was reveling in the beauty of the newly envisioned mechanics of the cell membrane. A few heartbeats later I was overtaken by a joy so deep and wide, my heart ached and tears flowed from my eyes. The mechanics of the new science revealed the existence of our spiritual essence and our immortality. For me, the conclusions were so unambiguous I instantly went from non-believer to believer. (183)

-...while science led me to my euphoric moment of insight, the experience resembled instantaneous conversions described by mystics. (184)

- Aboriginal cultures do not make the usual distinctions among rocks, air and humans; all are imbued with spirit, the invisible energy. Doesn't this sound familiar? This is the world of quantum physics, in which matter and energy are completely entangled. And it is the world of Gaia, a world in which the whole planet is considered to be one living, breathing organism.... (185)

- The fact that science led me to spiritual insight is appropriate because the newest discoveries in physics and cell research are forging new links between the worlds of Science and Spirit. These realms were split apart in the days of Descartes centuries ago. However, I truly believe that only when Spirit and Science are reunited will we be afforded the means to create a better world. (185)

We have quoted much from Bruce Lipton's story of progressive peak experiences because we deem his story a useful and powerful case study demonstrating many of the themes of this book. Peak experiences are moments of high elation bringing with them clear, experiential knowledge, (that is, a blending of head and heart 'knowing') that deeply affects individuals and, very often, brings about change for humanity as a whole. We also believe that this scientific 'aha moment', so well documented by Lipton, a gifted writer and teacher noted for the clarity of his presentations, may well become a model of the paradigm-shattering insights, the mountain-top moments, that are becoming and will continue to become more prevalent, not only in the world of science, but in all fields of human endeavor and human culture.

SUMMARY OF CHAPTER SEVEN

From the various Resistance Forces which tend to squelch and repress the natural proclivities of human nature to grow and mature, we selected four to consider in this chapter. By far the most pernicious and most significant is the 'rotten-to-the-core'/original sin dogma because of its all-pervasiveness throughout the Western world. Even though modern societies have, in most other respects, largely abandoned their religious roots and forms, what has been called "the depravity doctrine" is alive and thriving!

Also, the Jonah Complex increases our tendencies to settle for a level far below our potential. For various reasons, we humans are often afraid of success.

Thirdly, it is our inherent laziness, says Colin Wilson, that allows the Robot to take over significant areas of our lives while we 'sleep', at low levels of consciousness, usually unaware that higher levels not only exist, but are periodically beckoning to us through evolutionary thrusts.

Finally, specifically related to peak experiences, a fourth resistance force is our unwillingness to face a materialistic, scientifically-based society, still largely hostile to what is perceived as religious, supernatural experiences.

In the next chapter, we consider five positive ways to encourage and nurture peak experiences.

CHAPTER EIGHT

BUILD THE LADDER AND PEs WILL COME

The great news is: *We can create the conditions that invite peak experiences into our lives.* Abraham Maslow at first assumed that PEs were entirely gratuitous, were unearned, and were to be passively received with gratitude. Later, after much study of 'self-actualized' people, he began to realize that many of the subjects he studied lived in such a way that they were likely to have many 'mild' PEs, i.e. a good, happy, awake and alive life. He referred to this as "plateau living". Then, he noted that many of his students, by remembering PEs and reporting them to the class, would experience more of them, and would remember previously forgotten ones. He even began to give students advice for inviting PEs into their lives. (Maslow, 1971)

Most of today's authors and students in the field of altered states of human consciousness believe that there are many ways that we can build the field, plant the seeds, prepare the way, create conditions that invite transcendent, mountain-top experiences into our lives. We here list those we feel would be most helpful. We use the metaphor of a ladder because states of consciousness are most often perceived as existing in a hierarchy. We all want to get further "up", towards the top. There are only five rungs to the ladder we are suggesting; we now know that *all that is needed is a relatively small flip of the mind to make it receptive to higher altered states.* And, as the examples in this book attest, an ever-so-slight change in perception can often profoundly change our lives forever.

The five rungs on the ladder to mountaintop experiences are all based on the ancient spiritual adage: *What you think about grows.* Most recently this basic law of life and the mind has been referred to as the Law of Attraction which is described by its earliest and most eminent popularizers, Jerry and Esther Hicks in the Abraham books and tapes, as"That which is like unto itself is drawn."

If we would have peak experiences, or have them more often than we do, we need to ponder them and nurture the ground of our consciousness for them.

FIVE RUNGS ON THE LADDER TO THE MOUNTAINTOP

1. Become aware of any peak experiences you have had.
2. Ask for PEs to come to you.
3. Become your mind's manager.
4. Spend time enjoying nature and music.
5. Practice appreciation and gratitude.

———

1. Awareness of PEs.

Bring to mind any such experience(s). Remember any you have had in the past, and recognize current ones. We recall that Professor Maslow's graduate students not only remembered additional PEs as they recorded earlier ones, but actually received more in present time as they continued to dwell upon these events.

Review your life looking for such events. It may help to look for them one decade at a time: e.g. ages one to ten, eleven to twenty, etc. You may be surprised how many PEs you will remember. You may have relegated them to your "Unaware Box" for any of the resistance reasons listed in the last chapter. Think about your aha moments, your private epiphanies, times when you felt euphoric. Write them down. As you do, you will remember more of the details, and especially the feelings that you had during the experience.

Suggestion A) Keep a journal of your PEs. Add to the list as you think of them. A journal or notebook is a way of "anchoring" the subtle and elusive messages from our transpersonal side, from the right hemispheres of our brains as noted by brain researcher, Dr. Jill Taylor, in Chapter 11. The right brain, the source of our insights, does not speak in words, but in pictures and feelings; its insights have to be quickly grounded or they disappear as quickly as unrecorded dreams.

Suggestion B) Share them by talking about them. Find someone who will be open to such discussions. Studies indicate there are growing numbers of people who are open to, and more than willing to talk about, such experiences. Of course, you will choose your 'PE Partners' wisely. Test the waters first. (Imagine with me a world where there are as many "AHA" sharing groups as there are self-help groups where sufferers of various conditions gather to share their symptoms. It's probably coming. Googling on the internet "Aha Experiences", we will find almost 2 million references already).

> "What! Have you felt that too? I thought I was the only one."
> - C.S. Lewis, <u>Surprised By Joy</u>, preface

2. Ask for PEs to come to you.

Whether you believe in the supernatural, a personal God, a benevolent universe, angels, a Higher Self within, or just the power of suggestion, asking for what you want is a powerful tool that is recommended by virtually all the leaders of the proven self-help methods.

3. Become your mind's manager.

Cultivate that part of your mind known as the Witness or the Observer.

A mind not aware of itself – ordinary consciousness – is like a passenger strapped into an airplane seat, wearing blinders, ignorant of the nature of transportation, the dimension of the aircraft, its range, the flight plan, and the proximity of other passengers.

The mind aware of itself is the pilot. True, it is sensitive to flight rules, affected by weather, and dependent on navigation aids, but still vastly freer than the 'passenger' mind.

Anything that draws us into a mindful, watchful state has the power to transform, and anyone of normal intelligence can undertake such a process. Mind, in fact, is its own transformative vehicle, inherently prepared to shift into new dimensions if only we let it. Conflict, contradiction, mixed feelings, all the elusive material that usually swirls around the edges of awareness can

be reordered at higher and higher levels. Each new integration makes the next easier.

This consciousness of consciousness, this witness level, is sometimes referred to as a 'higher dimension' which simply means a more inclusive dimension." – Marilyn Ferguson, The Aquarian Conspiracy, p. 69)

"The great lesson of the true mystics ... (is that) the sacred is in the ordinary, that It is to be found in one's daily life, in one's neighbors, friends and family, in one's backyard, and that travel may be a flight from confronting the sacred...To be looking elsewhere for miracles is a sure sign of ignorance that everything is miraculous.
-Abraham Maslow, (quoted in Hoffman, The Right to Be Human, pp. 331, 332)

THOUGHTS ON STEP THREE - MANAGING YOUR MIND

The most cursory examination of the literature on altered state peak experiences clearly indicates the universal importance of learning to control one's mind. For centuries, both eastern and western spiritual traditions have maintained that meditation is the royal road to mind taming, which leads to true happiness and personal power. The virtues of meditation are extolled by virtually every spiritual author and authority as the primary method to achieve this.

Modern science has begun to consider the scientific evidence for the values of meditation. During the 1970s, the technique called Transcendental Meditation was extensively studied at Harvard University. A landmark book, published in 1975, The Relaxation Response, by Harvard's chief meditation researcher, Dr.

Hugh Benson, became a best seller. Benson expounded on the large number of scientifically-proven benefits of twenty-minute-daily meditation cycles, not only using the method called Transcendental Meditation (TM) but *using any method* that included the four steps listed below. The steps, by the way, describe and define active meditation, focusing the mind on one object; passive meditation strives to clear all thoughts, emotions and perceptions from the mind.

1. A quiet place.
2. A comfortable position.
3. An object to dwell upon, e.g. one's breathing or repeating a word or phrase. (Many people find that 'dwelling upon' one's breathing has many physiological and psychological benefits.)
4. An attitude of passive acceptance of whatever thoughts or feelings arise.

Hundreds of studies since Benson's books (he also wrote several sequels) have found the same general conclusion: *many highly significant positive effects for our body-minds can be produced by meditating, even for short periods.*

All of the research on meditation agrees: Meditation is one of the nicest things you can do for yourself. Read how science writer Dawson Church puts it in his 2007 <u>The Genie in Your Genes: Epigenetic Medicine and the New Biology of Intention</u>:

The health benefits of meditation are well documented and numerous. Meditation has been shown to lower blood pressure, improve resting heart rate, reduce the incidence of strokes, heart disease and cancer, diminish chronic pain, ameliorate anxiety and depression, and have a beneficial effect on many other diseases. *If meditation were a drug, it would be considered medical malpractice for a physician to fail to prescribe it.* ... A single brief period of spiritual and

emotional centering in the morning affects our immune system all day long and sets us up for a healthier and more peaceful emotional baseline.

(p. 155) (Italics added)

In his 2009 book, <u>Embracing the Wild Sky: a Tour Across the Horizons of the Mind</u>, autistic savant Daniel Tammet tells of a very recent study that shows a relationship of peak experiences and meditation. A group of ten college students, quickly taught the rudiments of meditation, were compared to eight Buddhist monks who had had many years of practice in meditation. All the subjects were wired to electroencephalographs and were examined via MRIs as both groups meditated on the virtue of compassion – opening up to feelings of unlimited love and generosity towards all living beings.

There were interesting differences between the monks and the novices. The monks' brains showed much greater activity in regions of the brain associated with empathy and maternal love. And when the monks were generating feelings of compassion, activity in the part of the brain associated with negative feelings was swamped by activity in the area correlated with happiness. In contrast, the students' brains showed no such activity.

In each instance, the monks with the most hours of meditation showed the most significant brain changes, supporting the idea that mental training can make the brain more prone to states of happiness, compassion, and empathy. According to this evidence, being happy is a skill that you can train yourself to learn. That is certainly one beautiful thought worth meditating on. (p. 18)

BARRIERS TO MIND MANAGEMENT - RESISTANCE TO MEDITATION

Most of us are by now quite aware that meditation and centering, i.e., periods of quiet relaxation while pondering some positive, or at least neutral subject, are very good for us and we would be well advised to do it regularly. However, many of us (present author included) experience serious resistance to the daily practice of meditative techniques. Most of us just don't do it! We find myriad excuses not to perform this relatively simple, yet onerous task.

This resistance to meditation has been observed by many. Researcher Charles Tart estimates after discussions with some of the most recognized teachers of meditation such as Shinzen Young, that barely five percent of those who learn meditative practices actually continue the practice! Tart admits his own problems: "I'd been given meditation instructions by a number of teachers over the years and, until I met Shinzen, I'd long ago decided that whatever special talent it took to be a meditator, I didn't have it, so I'd given it up." (The End of Materialism, p. 325)

Another example: Dr. James Nourse is a clinical psychologist and acupuncturist in practice for over 30 years. He writes the following pertinent 'confession' in his 2008 book, Simple Spirituality: Finding Your Own Way. (His book, as we will see – like many books – is itself the result of a peak or plateau experience.)

I can't even remember how many times I have started, and stopped, meditating. I have taught my clients how to meditate, and have sent them to formal meditation classes and they often sheepishly admit after a few weeks that they haven't meditated in a while. I know exactly what they are experiencing, because I have gone through the same thing. There are many reasons for it, but, for whatever reason, other demands displace spiritual practice. The unfortunate consequence is that most people feel a sense of shame and failure about it, think they are too weak or undisciplined or

that their problems or responsibilities as just too big to allow them to have a spiritual life. I know. (p. 10)

But one morning Nourse had what I describe as a highly significant life and world changing "plateau experience" of enlightened knowledge while driving to work. He was on his way to his office in Brevard, a small mountain town in North Carolina.

It was a cool, gray spring morning with a gentle rain falling. I slipped a disc of quiet selections into the CD player and leaned back to spend the next half hour waking up enough to begin a day of seeing clients. I can't say exactly when I became aware of it, but at some point I had found my way into a feeling of utter contentment. The grayness of the morning, the lushness of the earth, the metronome of the windshield wipers, the gently rhythms of the music and the steady movement of the scenery and I as the observer of it all *became woven into one fabric, one substance, one mind. I can't say there was any drama in it at all, no great joy, no profound thoughts, no visions or voices. Just a feeling of utter contentment.*

Later into the drive I became aware that I was no longer wholly in the experience, but was beginning to *think about* the experience. <u>What came to me is that this is the way I want to feel in all aspects of my life, that this is the essence of a spiritual life, finding that sort of deep contentment and connection in the very everydayness of life</u>. ...

What I realized in this simple experience was that *spirituality is just a different 'take' on the scenery we wind our way through every ordinary day.* What if we could cultivate the capacity for experiencing life in this way, rather than just waiting and hoping for it to happen?" (pp. 7-8) (Underlining added)

Dr. Nourse, and many teachers like him, point out ways we can bring that enlightened attitude to ordinary life, ways we can cultivate an attitude of conscious awareness that will change our lives. We seek nothing less that the development of a state of awakened consciousness. As William James, the father of American psychology, said many years ago, the slightest shift in perception, a change of focus, is all that is needed to be ushered into a new and profound appreciation and acceptance of reality, what Nourse calls, "the scenery we wind our way through every ordinary day."

On The Miracle of Mindfulness

Our true home is in the present moment.
To live in the present moment is a miracle.
The miracle is not to walk on water.
The miracle is to walk on the green earth in the present moment,
to appreciate the peace and beauty that are available now.
Peace is all around us-
In the world and in nature-
And within us – in our bodies and our spirits.
Once we learn to touch this peace
We will be healed and transformed.
It is not a matter of faith.
It is a matter of practice.

Thich Nhat Hanh (from The Miracle of Mindfulness)

So, we are advised to practice being aware and awake to our true home, the present moment. "Being awake", according to Dr. Nourse, "is doing something and knowing that you are doing it, thinking something and knowing that you are thinking it, feeling something and knowing what you are feeling." (p 20)

Does it not seem ironic that the third rung of our ladder to the higher consciousness which invites transpersonal peak experiences is to pay attention to, even to immerse oneself in, the mundane, 'ordinary' moments of our time and place in the world in which we presently live? This, of course, is how we wrest control from the robot of Chapter 7, who, in serving us all too well, sucks the vitality and joy out of life.

---

4. Enjoy nature and music whenever possible.

Nature and music are two of the most often named "triggers" of peak experiences throughout the world. Go often to attractive natural surroundings. Try to just 'be there' without thinking. Listen often to music that you love. Let sound move you, not just emotionally, but physically; sway with it, dance to it.

> Spend all you have for loveliness,
> Buy it and never count the cost;
> For one white singing hour of peace
> Count many a year of strife well lost,
> And for a breath of ecstasy
> Give all you have been, or could be.
>
> -Sara Teasdale

5. Appreciate the 'miracles' here and now in your life.

Set aside a few minutes each day to consider your many gifts, however you define them. Medical psychologist Dan Baker recommends that we conduct an Appreciation Audit three times a day (upon awakening, at midday meal and before bed). The author and his wife share the day's good things that happened, "miracles," before sleep each night so that the subconscious mind can mull them over while the body sleeps. We have noted that if we are peaceful and positive as we fall asleep, the morning will begin much brighter.

EXAMPLE OF PLATEAU LIVING: A LUMINOUS EXPERIENCE OF GRATITUDE

Abraham Maslow noted that 'self-actualized' people, successful, happy people from every socio-economic class and background, often seemed to live very satisfying lives on high emotional, cultural and spiritual levels. Such persons seem to have a mental attitude of joy and serenity which, like a lighthouse beacon, attracts and entrains others. Such individuals usually have many transcendental moments in their lives; Maslow termed this 'plateau living'.

A recent example of a peak experience capping a life spent on a high plateau of selfless service involved one of America's leading symphony orchestras, the Buffalo (NY) Philharmonic, as it publicly recognized a 25 year relationship with one of its Associate Conductors, Dr. Paul Ferington. "Dr. Paul" fully fits Maslow's description of self–actualized. He exudes zest for living and has many friends and admirers. He successfully melded two professional careers. His 'day job' involved teaching music and holding various administrative positions at a community college, including Vice President of Academic Affairs. He retired from this college career in 2006.

While pursuing his challenging academic career (as well as raising a family), Dr. Paul, because he loved music and loved conducting, offered his services at no cost to the Buffalo Philharmonic Orchestra (BPO). Since he was a highly qualified classical pianist and conductor, the BPO enthusiastically accepted this offer and a relationship began that has lasted more than 25 years. "Over the past 25 years", Ferington says, "I have donated all my services and never taken a fee; in addition to conducting 421 concerts at 61 different locations since 1985, in 2004 I created an "Adult Music Appreciation Series", lectures designed to preview upcoming concerts for audience members."

For the 25th anniversary in 2010, unbeknownst to Dr. Paul, an elaborate celebration was being arranged by the musicians. At a gala event celebrated annually for the donors to the orchestra, a most unusual surprise was presented to Dr. Paul. A year before, the musicians had commissioned a special piece of music to be composed for, and dedicated to, this long-standing associate conductor who had achieved such a milestone - a quarter century of extraordinary service! The brilliant young composer chosen for this task was Christopher Rogerson. As a surprise tribute to Dr. Paul, the orchestra, conducted by Principal Conductor JoAnn Falletta, performed the world premier of this work, titled "Luminosity for Orchestra." The composer's dedication of the piece was read to the audience:

The musicians of the BPO approached me in 2009 about possibly commissioning a concert opener in honor of Paul Ferington's 25 years on the BPO Conducting Staff. I was thrilled by the offer. Paul has been a great mentor and friend to me….he is one of those rare people whose joy for life is contagious to every person around him. The result is a celebratory piece for Paul…and it was to be "fittingly joyous"! Thus came *Luminosity* – a portrait of the light and excitement Paul exudes.

Dr. Paul, writing shortly after the event, was still in a state of stunned amazement. "The gift from the musicians is magic enough and so many have commented, 'This type of thing NEVER happens from Orchestral players'. The concept that they began planning this surprise honor over a year ago is overwhelming; but the fact that the composer wrote every measure of this work as a musical tribute to, and in honor of me, is still numbing and surreal!"

———

<u>SUMMARY OF CHAPTER EIGHT</u>   *The five steps, all geared to greater awareness of the positives in life, are meant to prepare the field, to plant the seeds for relatively happy, peaceful, fulfilling plateau living - a manner of living that creates the conditions for the occurrence of peak experiences into our lives.*

1. **BECOME AWARE OF PEAK EXPERIENCES IN YOUR LIFE, BOTH THOSE OF THE PAST AND OF THE PRESENT. RECORD THEM IN WRITING AND TALK TO OTHERS ABOUT THEM.**
2. **ASK FOR MORE ENLIGHTENMENT MOMENTS TO COME TO YOU.**
3. **BECOME THE MANAGER OF YOUR OWN MIND THROUGH MEDITATION AND/OR YOUR AWARENESS OF THE PRESENT MOMENT.**
4. **SPEND TIME ENJOYING NATURE AND MUSIC.**
5. **PRACTICE APPRECIATION AND GRATITUDE.**

In chapter nine, Towards Understanding PEs, we will present some theories and ideas to help us understand how PEs come about and why they are so important.

WIRED FOR THE TRANSCENDENT

To many religionists it may seem ironic that an avowed atheist, Abraham Maslow, not only coined the word, "peak experience", but spearheaded the scientific study and exploration of altered states and the "farther reaches of human nature" (the title of one of his books). The fact is that as soon as one begins to explore "the farther reaches", one is very quickly immersed in the mysteries of transcendence – higher states of consciousness, spirituality, the realm of religion. It has been pointed out many times that the human brain seems to be wired for the transcendent.

As spiritual author John Shelby Spong, retired Episcopal Bishop, expressed it in a recent autobiographical reference, "I was becoming a religious roamer....this is what human beings have always been. I was really replicating in my individual life the history of my species. *It is the nature of self-conscious life to cope with the issues of meaning and mortality by engaging in a religious search."* (Eternal Life: A New Vision, 2009, p.52)

We have seen in an earlier chapter (Day and Night: The Language of Reason and Reverence), that the vast majority of the world's reported PEs speak, however falteringly, of exalted states of consciousness and often refer – depending on the specific background of the peakers - to deities and angels, to remarkable unearthly beings and supernatural visitations. It is no surprise, then, that religion and its scriptures, practices, rituals, devotions and prayers have occasioned immense numbers of PEs.

Some examples follow. We have arbitrarily divided them into four groups:

A. Sacred Places
B. Scripture
C. Miracles of healing
D. Meditation and prayer.

A. SACRED PLACES

Many religions honor places that are perceived as sacred either because of certain historical events that have occurred there or because there is certain power felt there. Lourdes in France is a well-known example in recent history. The ancient philosophies and practices of dowsing and geomancy have always recognized that certain spots on the earth are power spots where, for example, energy (ley) lines cross. Often these were, and/or continue to be the sites of sacred shrines. Other examples include Stonehenge in England, Delphi in Greece, the site of the pyramids, the vortexes (power spots) around Sedona, Arizona, as well as the sites of many, if not most, of the great cathedrals and pilgrimage destinations of the world.

─────────

The Power Center of Chartres Cathedral

The most profound peak experience of my life happened in 1983 when I went on a peace pilgrimage led by Alan Cohen (spiritual author and leader). Our intention was to celebrate joyfully the presence of peace in the places we visited. We traveled across Europe, following the ley lines and visiting major power centers and ancient pilgrimage sites, praying for world peace at each one.

The trip itself was a peak experience, but one particular place stood out for me, the Cathedral of Chartres in France. As we approached on the bus from about ten miles away, I began to feel a very loving energy pulsing and gathering around my heart. As we drove by the cathedral, our guide explained that this beautiful cathedral had burned to the ground several centuries after it was built, and was rebuilt a few centuries later.

For reasons that I don't recall, I did not go on the tour of the cathedral with the rest of the group. I arrived about an hour later, and encountered our guide in the vestibule of the cathedral. He had finished the tour with the rest of the group, but he took me to a spot in the vestibule, and asked me to close my eyes and meditate there. The energy was so strong that it nearly knocked me over!

The guide explained that normally the high altar of a church was built over the power center, a dome well, where power emanated from the earth and drew energy down from the heavens. After the cathedral burned, the memory of the power center apparently was lost, and the high altar was located in a different place. Where I was standing and meditating was the power center, right there in the vestibule of the church where hundreds of people walked over it every day! I stayed there for a long time, meditating and absorbing the wonderful, powerful heart energy.

I walked back to the inn where we were staying. My roommate, Grace, was lying in one of the twin beds meditating. I lay on the other bed, and we linked our hands and began to meditate together. *When I closed my eyes, I began to see visions of many, many people of every age and description. These were people I did not know. They were peasants and merchants, priests and nuns, children and elders. They came one by one into my vision, and I realized that they were praying. An inner voice told me that these were all the people from every country who had ever prayed for peace. I had such an incredible feeling of oneness. I lingered in this vision and this feeling for a long time.*

At last the vision ended and I came out of the meditation. I asked Grace if she had seen the vision too, and she said she had. She said that during it, she received the awareness of total innocence joined with total wisdom.

This experience is a touchstone for me. As I write, I am re-experiencing it, and it helps me to remember that in Truth we are all one with everyone, whether living on the planet now, or living in a spiritual realm, and our spiritual dedication and purpose bind us together.

- Allaurah Olson, retired minister

THOMAS MERTON AND THE BUDDHIST STATUES

Thomas Merton, certainly the most famous modern monk of the Western world (1915 - 1968), spent seven hours a day for 27 years in formal prayer at the Trappist monastery of Gethsemani in

Kentucky. The author of <u>Seven Storey Mountain</u> and many other books on spiritual topics, Merton, in 1968, accepted an invitation to visit the East where he led retreats, met the Dalai Lama, and studied Buddhism. While there, he had the most profound peak experience of his life while viewing Buddhist statues in Sri Lanka, just a few days prior to his accidental death in Bangkok. The world learned of this event years later when his diary, <u>The Asian Journal,</u> was published.

Merton speaks of the silence and the solemnity as he, barefoot, approaches the Buddhas at the place of viewing.

For the doctrinaire, the mind that needs well established positions, such peace, such silence can be frightening. I was knocked over with a rush of relief and thankfulness at the obvious clarity of the figures, the clarity and fluidity of shape and line, the design of the monumental bodies composed into the rock shape and landscape. Looking at these figures I was suddenly, almost forcibly, jerked clean out of the habitual, half-tied vision of things, and an inner clearness, clarity, as if exploding from the rocks themselves, became evident and obvious. The thing about all this is that there is no puzzle, no problem, and really no 'mystery'. All problems are resolved and everything is clear, simply because what matters is clear. *The rock, all matter, all life, is charged with dharmakaya. Everything is emptiness and everything is compassion. I don't know when in my life I have ever had such a sense of beauty and spiritual validity running together in one aesthetic illumination.* (Italics added)

Surely my Asian pilgrimage has come clear and purified itself. I mean, I know and have seen what I was obscurely looking for. I don't know what else remains but I have now seen and have pierced through the surface and have got beyond the shadow and the disguise. This is Asia in its pu-

rity. It is clear, pure, complete. It says everything; it needs nothing. And because it needs nothing, it can afford to be silent, unnoticed, undiscovered. It does not need to be discovered. It is we, Asians included, who need to discover it. (Merton, The Asian Journal , pp. 233-237)

Vortexes of Sedona, Arizona

In 1991, the author of this book, while driving along one of the vortexes of Sedona, felt the clear, unmistakable presence of my father, who had been dead for 15 years. The emotional overlay of this experience was extremely positive and uplifting, and so strong that I had to pull over to the side of the road until I was able to compose myself. Tears flowed copiously. I was totally overcome with joy.

Machu Picchu, Peru

In 1943 the great Chilean poet Pablo Neruda climbed to Peru's lost city of Machu Picchu. As he wrote in his 1945 poem 'The Heights of Machu Picchu,' there he discovered 'the old and unremembered human heart.' All at once he felt compassion for the human race and dedicated the rest of his life to the poor and oppressed. On the mountain he had a spiritual experience and received a mission that he spent the rest of his life trying to fulfill.   (Quoted from John Dear's Transfiguration, p. 45)

Mesa Verde, Arizona

The following account of a two-part sacred site experience comes from a woman in her fifties. Ann is a student of the Huna philosophy and a counselor.

It began on a spring day in the mid-nineties. I had flown into Durango, Colorado, from St. Louis, Missouri. I had never been west of the Rockies before. I had rented a car to drive to Dolores, about an hour away. The scenery in that part of Colorado was breathtaking: snow-topped peaks of the San Juan Mountains shading into the jagged mesas surrounding Mesa Verde National Park. *As I rounded a curve I saw a huge mesa partially superimposed on a mountain-top range, clearly a sight beyond the senses. The energy was so strong I had to stop the car and stare. I was immersed in the sight and the energy that drew me so strongly. It was very clear to me that everything had changed - my life could never be the same again. I must return – I had to be there!*

The second part of this experience occurred eight years later when I had the opportunity to move to that area. I bought a house that overlooked a pasture. Of all the houses I looked at with the realtor, I knew that this one was "my house". I didn't know why, but I acted on the feeling and bought the house.

The first time I stood on the patio, I saw, not the pasture, but hundreds of teepees – and I was there, part of life there! I don't know how long the experience lasted, but I know that I had been allowed to step into another dimension, to re-visit a place that had had a significant influence on who I am today. I know clearly that I am still linked to that lifetime; I am "tearing up" as a I write about it.

I later discovered that there had been a population of some 30,000 people in that area, the 'ancient Ones' known to us as the Anasazi.

This peak experience changed my life completely. While I lived there (near Mesa Verde) I was blessed to be able to feel my roots while working both at the National Park and at a technical college nearby. Working with Native Americans was a highlight of the whole experience. My heart is filled with gratitude.

- Ann Puryear (Italics added)

Throughout recorded history, sacred places have always been a significant part of man's life. Most religions, whether ancient or modern, began or evolved at special sites where a specific revelation was given to the founder. Jerusalem and Mecca; Rome and the Pantheon; Mount Sinai and Mount Tabor – are just a few places whose influence on religion are remarkable. Centuries ago Plato put it this way: "In all such qualities, those places excel in which there is a divine inspiration, and in which the gods have their appointed lots and are propitious to the dwellers in them."

We will not be surprised, then, to find voluminous peak experiences connected with such places. Indeed, the high tops of mountains have always been recognized for their numinous qualities; a synonym for PEs is mountain-top experiences.

B. SCRIPTURES

To the devotees of myriad religions, even more important than sacred places are certain writings, especially if attributed to the religion's founder or early followers of the founder. Most often, these writings are considered the very Word of God, transmitted by a divine inspiration to the writers and, therefore, enjoying a remarkable degree of authenticity and authority, even after being translated into various languages. Add to this the fact that over the centuries (for older religions) millions of adherents have been adding the power of their thought forms to the field each time that they read or think about these writings.

We will expect, then, to have many peak experiences associated with the reading of the various Scriptures.

LIVING WATER

In 1980, I was at a Siddha Yoga Ashram in New York State for the first time. I was in a large meditation hall amongst many devotees chanting Sanskrit words. I didn't know the meaning of the words, but the chanting and the meditation that followed felt right and so very good.

Suddenly something "bopped" me on the head. I whipped around to see what had hit me. There was nothing there, but in that moment I felt energy rushing up my spine. *I felt a joy I had never felt before. And I had an instantaneous understanding of Christian scripture I had been familiar with all my life*, especially John 4:13 where Jesus told the Samaritan woman at the well, "Everyone who drinks of this water will thirst again, but whoever drinks of the water that I shall give him will never thirst; the water that I shall give him will become in him a spring of water welling up to eternal life."

At that moment I <u>knew</u> this scripture, and many other passages that came rushing through me, with a new understanding, as if from the inside out. I felt as if I understood everything I had ever wondered about. All wisdom and knowledge was open to me. Everything was O.K. and I was filled with incredible joy. I felt light and larger than life, and one with everything there and everyone everywhere. I just wanted to dance, hug trees and laugh.

Later I was told that I had just received "Shaktipat", that is, the awakening of my inner being/Kundalini. The Kundalini had been awakened and had risen through my spine from base to the top of my head.

During that same weekend, my Guru, Gurumayi, gave me a spiritual name. I had not told her of my peak experience. When I approached her at Darshan (a time for individuals to greet the Guru) and asked for a name, she took a name card out of a box, looked at me, shook her head, and put it back into the box. She withdrew another name, nodded, smiled, and gave it to me. My spiritual name? It is Smirti which means, "one who has knowledge of spiritual law."

Whatever happened that day was truly a peak experience I shall never forget.

- Romella Hart

WORLD UNITY AND PEACE – BAHA' I FAITH

The Baha'i faith, only about 150 years old, is one of the world's fastest growing religions with over five million followers. The essential message of the Baha'is that of unity. There is only one God, one human race. All the world's religions represent stages in the revelation of God's will and purpose for humanity. In our day, mankind has come of age; the time has arrived for the unifying of all peoples into a peaceful and integrated global society.

Baha'i member Jane Wilder, while reading from the writings of the founder, Baha u llahirte, in 2010 was overcome with the memory of a PE that occurred years before while she was attending a World Congress.

> I recalled the first morning of the Baha' i World Congress held in New York City in 1992. The Convention Hall at the Jacob K. Javits Center was filled twice for each session with Baha' is from all over the world. The choir and orchestra brought together people who had practiced the music in their own communities and combined to make the most heavenly music. As I listened to the words, "Rejoice, rejoice, the Promised Day has come", I really felt my heart would burst with joy. Here we were, manifesting God's Words for this time, that we all must unify the human race in love and harmony and bring about His promise of world peace. As I recall that time again, the tears are rolling down my cheeks.

LOVE OF GOD, NEIGHBOR AND SELF

Walter Starke is a well-known retreat leader and author of spiritual books including his 2006 work, Joel Goldsmith and I, about his close relationship with Goldsmith, also a well known writer and modern mystic. In a recent issue of his newsletter, Starke writes of a profound peak experience many years ago which, he now realizes, contained keys to understanding and appreciating the very modern concept of globalization. It is an apt illustration of the timelessness that characterizes most PEs.

> Personally, the seeds of ultimate globalization were planted in my own consciousness over fifty years ago. While sitting on the rim of the Haleakala Crater in Hawaii, I had what

would qualify as an epiphany that revealed what I now see as the key to spiritual globalization.

At that moment I saw that the unappreciated or unrecognized secret hidden in Jesus' message was that he proposed the acceptance and reconciliation of an apparent duality in order for us to achieve a true oneness.

I saw that Jesus' instructions for us to equally love both the invisible source of our creativity (God) and also its visible material manifestation (neighbor and self) meant for us to equally appreciate both cause and effect; and if we could love both, it would not only put an end to exclusivity and duality but would also reveal that they were just different expressions of the same reality, two sides of one coin.

When I had that revelation, I had no idea that in my lifetime Jesus' seemingly simple instruction would relate to globalization and the biggest collective transformation the world has ever experienced. Now almost sixty years later, I realize that Jesus' two thousand-year-old advice also included the solution to what is finally becoming undeniable evident as the way to achieve both a spiritual and humanly harmonious globalization.

Globalization is another word for oneness and in that respect spiritual "sameness." We can't have a total anything and leave something out. The truth is not either/or, but both/and. All people on earth have been cut from the same cloth.

(Starke, "Circle Letter", Winter 2009, p. 7)

ASK AND YOU SHALL RECEIVE

One morning, as I sat writing a little book on affirmations, papers and books spread before me at the dining room table, I began concentrating on the word "ask". Suddenly, in a flash, I noticed that the letters of the word were the first three letters of the biblical teaching, "Ask and ye shall receive, Seek and ye shall find, Knock and it shall be opened unto you." How interesting!

As I sat with intense focus and concentration, while pondering the word "ask", suddenly I was in another dimension that was not physical. I had no body. There were no "things". It was a space of thought only. I *knew* what the word "ask" meant. I knew without words. I had complete understanding of immense concept and meaning.

I was euphoric. It felt like an unending spiritual orgasm. I floated in exhilarated understanding of immeasurable depth and felt such joy, such bliss, that words cannot touch. My heart was fully open. This understanding was not in my mind. My mind wasn't present. There were no words, no mental activity at all. I was *living* the knowledge. It was infinite space, infinite knowledge about the concept of "ask". There were no boundaries, no limitations, only complete awareness, complete joy.

It was timeless, going on and on. In reality, I don't know how much worldly time passed. In some tiny part of my mind, I became aware that I was experiencing this bliss, and with this mental observation, the oneness of knowing began to fade. As I began to return to mental comprehension, I felt great sorrow. I wanted to stay "there".

I tried to hold onto the feeling of bliss and oneness with "knowing", but the more I tried, the more it faded. I felt a terrible sadness and longing to return to that blissful state. I felt bereft and empty. Desperately, I tried to retain everything I had learned by putting it into words. Words failed to capture it. I was losing so much of what I had understood, lived. I was left with what felt like empty words. It was terribly painful, an unbelievable loss.

I would never recapture that experience, nor another one like it. Now, it is painful to try to explain the meaning of the word "ask" because I feel so painfully inadequate and the word had such immense depth, far beyond the mind's ability to grasp.

Having had this experience, I *know* there is far more to life than what we see, feel and think. And I *know* that I experienced only the minutest of immeasurably greater and unlimited knowledge and bliss. In my darkest hours, I am comforted beyond measure in knowing that the time will come when I will live in that blissful "knowing" for all time. There is nothing greater.

- Suka Chapel

PROGRESSIVE GUIDANCE – THE BEGINNING:

Christian minister Jeanne L. McCoy knew very early that she was 'called' to a life of service centering around the Bible. Now in her seventies, she has never pastored a church but has served in many ministerial capacities. She has recently returned from six weeks in Africa ministering to church leaders and congregations. Periodically throughout her life, she reports receiving clear messages guiding her into a life of intense study of Sacred Scripture.

These messages came via mountain-top experiences taking various forms. She is writing a book about her "wonderful, happy life serving the Lord". What follows is an excerpt from her forthcoming book.

She tells us of living as an eight year old child in Hopewell, Virginia, and being introduced there to the man named Jesus by a teacher in a nearby Moravian one-room church. She first experienced the warmth of the Christian people there. "…I began to have a sense of longing, a strange emotion that continued even after we moved the following summer, back to Charlottesville, Virginia, where I had been born." In June of 1952 she attended Vacation Bible School at a Southern Baptist church on the campus of the University of Virginia.

We sang, learned Bible stories and delighted in making craft items to take home. Each day we gathered in the sanctuary for the closing of the day's activities.

As the pastor was talking, I suddenly lost awareness of things around me but was acutely aware of being enclosed in a bubble, face to face with the man, Jesus. Instantly I was flooded with an intense awareness of his love for me even though we did not speak aloud. My next awareness was standing before the pastor to tell him, "I love Jesus". To my surprise, I had walked down the formerly fearful long red carpeted aisle. I stayed with my pastor for a few minutes after the group was dismissed so that we could read the scriptures he selected. I was scheduled to be baptized in water within two weeks.

I was in love for the first time. The days seemed filled with sunshine. There were silver linings around the clouds and all of nature seemed alive and new to me. I seemed to be seeing everything with a new set of eyes. My cousins wanted to hear how it felt to be born again and I tried to explain.

It is now 58 years since my introduction to Jesus. While I have not understood every event in my life, I have never lost the assurance I have of the unconditional love Jesus has for me.

C. Healings

Healings, whether spontaneous or 'more natural', are often associated with changes in states of consciousness and mountain top experiences. Some authorities of the spiritual life maintain that only with a change in consciousness does any real and lasting physical or emotional healing occur. We begin our examples with the healing of Judith Pennington who went on to become a well known author and coast-to-coast teacher of meditation techniques that use computer programs.

Even as a child, I sensed the sacred light in nature and in my mystical Catholic church. In my teenage years I rejected religion and forgot the feeling of light. But one morning in 1974, I experienced God in an unforgettable way.

While driving to a follow-up medical examination, I instinctively sent up a heartfelt prayer for help, and in that split second, a cold chill swept over my body and changed into a sensation of warm, radiant bliss. Cascading waves of light aroused joy and ecstasy. The light steadily intensified and I overflowed with gratitude. Weeping in joy and wonder, I knew this to be the light of God and how it feels to die.

In a very real sense, I did die in those 20 minutes of radiant bliss, as I was never the same again. It wasn't the healing of the large growth on my ovary, but the memory of how the healing had felt that stunned me. Now I knew that God existed and I wanted more than anything else to live in that radiant light.

(Pennington, "The Meditation Experience", Venture Inward, Jan/Feb 2009, p.15)

Sometimes a healing does not occur immediately when the PE happens, but, instead, takes time, and perhaps effort, to take hold and manifest in the physical domain. A celebrated example of this is the case of Myrtle Fillmore, the co-founder (with her husband, Charles Fillmore) of Unity Church, one of the New Thought movements that arose in the 19th century in the United States.

Myrtle's health was declining rapidly when the watershed peak event happened. She had been diagnosed with tuberculosis, a condition that also affected others in her family. After much doctoring, she was told that nothing further could be done and was given just six months to live. She was 42 years old.

In the spring of 1886, she and Charles, living at the time in Kansas City, Missouri, attended a New Thought lecture given by a Chicago metaphysical teacher, Dr. E. B. Weeks. *During the lecture, Myrtle reacted in a profound and life-changing manner to one sentence uttered by the speaker: "I am a child of God and therefore I do not inherit sickness". That sentence changed her life. Along with the study of metaphysical principles, Myrtle hourly and daily repeated the child of God affirmation and used other techniques to heal herself.*

Rather than engaging another practitioner, she revealed many years later, "I did most of the healing myself, because I wanted the understanding for future use".

I began to claim my birthright and to act as though I believed myself the child of God, filled with His life. I gained. And others saw that there was something new in me. And they asked me to share it. I did. Others were healed, and began to study also. My husband continued his business,

and at first took little interest in what I was doing. But after a time he became absorbed in the study of Truth too.
(Vahle, <u>Torch-Bearer to Light the Way: The Life of Myrtle Fillmore</u>, p. 5)

The complete healing took about a year; her heath gradually improved and she went on to live until the age of 86. After a long, busy life lived in good health, Myrtle died in 1931. Her peak experience during the lecture in Kansas City not only saved her life, but was also the beginning of the world-wide Unity movement.

———

The two examples above, one spontaneous, one which took a year to complete, represent thousands of reported cases from every country, clime and circumstance. Healings are often the result of PEs which are palpable and striking.

———

The death of loved ones is a frequent trigger for peak experiences of healing. Sometimes the healing brings persons back from death's door; more often, however, deathbed PEs have to do with healing relationships during the final hours, or as in the case that follows, of reassuring and bringing peace to either the dying person or others involved.

AN UNALTERABLE PRESENCE

There was an evening several days before he passed away that I went to see my dad in the hospital. He had been suffering with terminal cancer of the pleura, or wall of his chest, for almost a year. My sister and I were spending as much time as possible with him at that time. The doctor had let us know that he did not have much time left.

By now his condition had worsened and he was unconscious most of the time. Even though he was unconscious, his body was restless with pain. His face grimaced even as he slept. I felt quite helpless to do much for him. I talked to him and held his hand in hope he might know I was there. I read for him a lesson from <u>A Course in Miracles</u>, as we were in the habit of doing, but he showed no acknowledgement of hearing it.

It was just after dark. His room was not bright, but was evenly illuminated. Suddenly, as I sat there quietly with him, and while in a frame of mind no different from that I was normally in, *there came into that room a feeling of such grace and depth and peace that I will never forget it. It was an absolutely unquestionable presence which no descriptive words could possibly do justice to.* I remember thinking that the only word which could even touch it was 'unalterable'. It was a presence with a tangible, almost physical nature. It had a feeling of such substance and viscosity that I felt that I could have reached out into thin air with a knife and sliced off chunks of it. *Although I couldn't see it, the presence was more real to me than anything in the room that I could see.*

The best part of it, however, was that it brought with it a 'knowing' that dad was just fine. I do not say this whimsically but with the certainty of knowing. Although dad lay before me, his body writhing with pain, I felt total joy for him. I *knew* he was just fine. This was not a fleeting occurrence. It stayed with me for the entire visit. I sat with him for a couple more hours until I had to leave for my midnight shift at the bakery. That feeling of certainty stayed with me as I left the hospital, got into my car and drove home to change my clothes.

That evening affected me more than I realized at the time. I had been raised very much believing in science and the power of the mind to understand all things. But this was beyond the mind! *For me, it was the evening where God went from being an idea in my mind to something I actually knew as real. This happened about 26 years ago, but I cannot recall the experience without being choked in tears for the power and the beauty of it.*

— Robert Ruhe

D. Meditation and Prayer

We begin this section with another teacher of meditation techniques, Anna Wise, who is considered a consciousness pioneer and is the author of two classic texts on meditation and brain wave development, <u>Awakening the Mind</u> and <u>The High Performance Mind.</u>

"The magnificence of light revealed itself to Anna Wise at age 16. She had been attending a church in Boulder, Colorado, and one day looked down at her bible and asked God to prove His existence. 'The sky opened up, a golden light came down, there were celestial choirs, and I was completely blissed out' for four hours, she said.
-"The Meditation Experience" by Judith Pennington,<u>Venture Inward</u>, Jan/Feb 2009)

A CENTERING PRAYER LEADS TO AN OUT-OF-BODY EXPERIENCE

It was an exciting day for me. It was 1992, two days after my 55th birthday and I was giving a recital at St. Paul's Episcopal Cathedral in Buffalo, New York. I was very nervous, so, before I began to sing, I said a centering prayer "It is not I, of myself, that does this singing, but the Presence within me that does this work." That prayer always seemed to "work" for me; after I said it, I could let myself sing with freedom.

The program began, and about halfway through I was singing "Un Bel Di" from Puccini's Madame Butterfly when, all of a sudden, I was flying above the floor of this great cathedral at the height of the top of the stained glass windows, looking down at the stone flooring and all the people sitting in the wooden pews! I felt a breeze and I was flying like a bird. I was music and music was me and I was the stone floor and the windows and the pews and the people. I felt gloriously light, alive, free, and at one with everything and everybody. I was tiny and immense at the same time, and then there was only glorious nothingness. Then I saw myself, below, and heard the sound of me singing. Whoosh. I was standing there singing. I finished the program in a daze. It was an amazing experience that I shall never forget.
- R. Hart

AN ACTOR'S EXPERIENCE WITH MEDITATION

Alan Arkin is a celebrated Oscar-recipient actor. In 1969, all was going very well for him. Successful in his career, his marriage thriving, "I had realized a life that would have been the envy of most people in the world. The one problem I could not work around was that I was angry and unhappy most of the time. I was all right when I was acting…but the rest of the time I was actively confused and empty."

Through a meeting with a new "stand-in" on a film set, Arkin met "John" who was to become his guru or spiritual guide. Through John, Arkin was introduced to Eastern spirituality and a form of yoga meditation. Arkin, like most westerners, was reluctant and distrustful at first, but gradually became aware that his life began to change significantly. His life took on an entirely new layer of meaning, and he was growing in happiness.

Arkin told his story in a 1979 book, <u>Halfway Through the Door: An Actor's Journey Toward the Self</u>. After meditating for some time, he began to notice shifts in his internal perceptions which led to one of the most significant peak experiences of his life which he well describes, using, of course, night language.

As I became more familiar with this wonderful feeling, something new happened. It was as if the top of my head was gently removed, cranium and brain, and I was plugged in directly to the Milky Way. The top of my head became a direct channel to a view of thousands of stars, and I was seeing them not with my eyes but with my entire consciousness, as if all my senses had merged, become one, and extended through the entirety of my body. This vision of harmony lasted perhaps five minutes, and when it was over I fell in love with myself. Sitting quietly and alone in a darkened room, I had given myself solace, joy and peace! It was the greatest imaginable gift… (p. 30)

What this one meditation did was hint to me that the peak experiences of my life, the transcendental moments on stage – which came, if I was lucky, once every few weeks for a few moments – these feelings were available all the time, every moment of my life. (p. 32)

<u>SUMMARY OF CHAPTER NINE</u>   *We have briefly explored a few examples of transcendent PEs, each representing thousands of similar events taking place throughout the world. PEs often occur at special places, hallowed and held sacred by various indigenous societies and/or religious or spiritual traditions. Also, PEs are often related to Sacred Scriptures, i.e., writings attributed to religious figures of the past. 'Miraculous' healings, which may be termed by scientists "spontaneous remissions", may occur along with PEs. A fourth category of causes or triggers for the transpersonal is spiritual practices, such as prayer, meditation, special rites and rituals, etc.*

In the concluding two chapters, we will discuss, briefly to be sure, ideas that may explain how and why these experiences occur.

TOWARDS UNDERSTANDING PEs

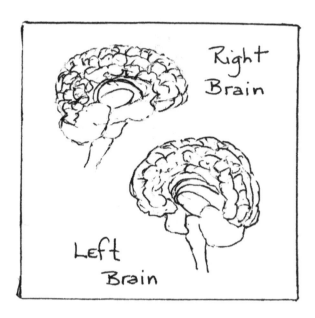

In this chapter we will explore, very briefly and cursorily to be sure, some ideas and theories that may shed some clarification on these "outbreaks of spirit" that continue to enlighten and enliven us humans. Also, we will make some important distinctions about the various levels of states of consciousness evoked by the somewhat loose term, 'peak experience'.

A- THE GESTALT HYPOTHESIS

We agree with most authors of the PE phenomena that, essentially, PEs are "knowledge explosions". During a peak experience, the experiencer _knows_ something beyond any doubt. The new learning, to use night language, is seared into his/her soul. It is experiential knowledge as compared to 'book learning'. It is heart understanding rather than mere head knowledge. It is 'knowledge plus'. It is 'Dr. Spock knowledge' with a powerful supercharged overlay of emotional content. The peaker *knows* that it is the truth for him or her; it can never be doubted.

The founder of Gestalt Psychology, Max Wertheimer, was a German philosopher and psychologist who was revered by Abraham Maslow as his most inspiring teacher. (Hoffman, <u>The Right To Be Human</u>, p.90) Wertheimer and two colleagues carried out many studies on human perception which emphasized the importance of "gestalts", or "wholes" in thinking and perceiving.

Wertheimer concluded that people learn, not through trial and error, as Behaviorists insisted, but through insight, a sudden perception, an "aha" experience. We learn through seeming 'revelations', a sudden seeing of a whole, a pattern that suddenly makes sense.

Wertheimer "insisted that deductive logic cannot possibly be the only, or even the most important, tool for knowledge in the world. He offered the analogy of a listener to a symphony. No amount of rational analysis of individual parts – violin, bassoon or drums – can reveal the design of a Beethoven symphony, yet hearing the whole makes the individual parts clear." (Ibid, p.91)

<u>We believe that most *PEs are gestalt experiences coming from "the farther reaches of human nature."*</u>

B - THE FILTER THEORY

From biology and psychology comes the filter theory, another help in explaining how we achieve altered states of consciousness.

Poet T.S. Eliot's well known dictum says "Human beings cannot bear too much reality". Because our brains and nervous systems need to be protected from excessive data rushing in all at once, nature has devised a system of filtering whereby we are fitted with restrictive barriers lest we be overwhelmed by the onrush of reality. (Scientists suggest that some kinds of mental abnormalities are caused when there is, for whatever reasons, a breakdown in the filtering system, as, for example, in certain forms of autism.)

Biologists point out that there are actually more brain cells designed to keep out data than there are that enable us to receive information from outside. These filters are repressive mechanisms calculated to impede the inrush of knowledge that would otherwise overwhelm and break us. In this sense, they are a sort of protective screen. The authors of the 2002 book, Natural Highs, conclude, "Our brains filter out the vast majority of information that comes in through our senses. This allows us to scan a mere fraction of what is actually out there and helps us to organize our world. We see only what we need to see for our survival." (Cass and Holford, p.165)

These protective barriers can sometimes be modified or removed. Sometimes they are removed by nature, as, for example when individuals are born with less restrictive filters. Some of these people we call 'psychics'; they are open to telepathy, clairvoyance and other parapsychological sources of information. Human beings have, since recorded history, found ways to soften these barriers so that we can enjoy out-of-the-ordinary experiences. The intake of drugs is clearly one way to affect the filters.

> William James spoke of the "thin veil" separating normal from altered states of consciousness. (11-4)

Some of the legal and less dangerous ways that we can soften the filters were discussed in Chapter 8. The best known of these is, of course, meditation, a gradual, health-generating process of giving attention to either the present moment or to one object, thereby restricting the rational consciousness from wandering. Meditation is highly recommended for safely and gradually opening the filters. More was said about this in Chapter 8.

C – THE HIGH SELF- ALL THE GOD WE CAN HANDLE?

The Huna philosophy, usually known through its Hawaiian/ Polynesian origins as re-discovered by Max Freedom Long (See bibliography), recognized the existence - long before Freud, Jung, or Assagioli - of three selves that live within each of us: the Basic Self, the Middle Self and the High Self. The author finds these concepts most helpful in attempting to explain peak experiences.

Huna is an ancient world view, a philosophy, a way of life, vestiges of which are common to many aboriginal people. Though much of it has been lost, it is generally viewed as more neutral, less ideological, less "religious" and, therefore, as coming with less controversial baggage than other approaches to explain reality.

An understanding of Huna's 'Trinity of Selves' can, hopefully, afford us a means to analyze, understand, and speak about these mountain-top experiences in a way that will spread light rather than heat.

The **Middle Self**, much like Dr. Spock of Star Wars fame, is completely rational and is the conscious control center, the self that speaks, reasons and decides. We normally think of it as the "I" of us.

The **Basic Self**, oriented to physical action and material things, is the seat of emotions and memory, and houses the five senses. It takes all language, even night language, literally, and has the mentality of a child/adolescent.

The **High Self**, of particular interest to the understanding of PEs, is the wise and loving source of inspiration, insight and absolute love. Normally inactive, except in emergencies or when asked by both of the other selves, the High Self is the perfect blend of masculine and feminine parental love, of right and left hemispheres of the brain. It is described as utterly trustworthy, as our link with the unknown and unknowable Divinity. It is, in the view of the Huna philosophy, all the "God" we humans can know and deal with, the source of the inspirations and 'divine nudges' that move us forward and bring us growth and joy.

When our High Self moves into active mode, whatever its rationale, a mountain-top experience occurs. We speculate that the three selves are, for the time that peak experience lasts (usually a very short time), at total attention, totally aligned, totally immersed in the unconditional love and unity that is the High Self's nature.

In our view, PEs do not arise from "supernatural" interventions, but from "the farther reaches of human nature," from the High Self, the highest and most evolved part of the human being. As Elmer Green, using a metaphor from the corporate business world, puts it, "(Each of us) individually as an ego, may be President of the Company, but the High Self is Chairman of the Board and determines goals and strategies." (The Ozawkie Book of the Dead: Alzheimer's Isn't What You Think It Is, p. 643)

Maslow seemed to be close to this understanding also. His biographer, Hoffman, says this: "Maslow also emphasized that each of us has an intrinsic core of personality – what he calls a 'real self' – unique and yet possessing traits in common with all humans. This core in not intrinsically evil, as the Freudians and theologians believe, but good or neutral." (p.15)

This is also the view of Marghanita Laski, the author of one of the earlier – and very excellent - compilations and studies of peak experiences, In the final sentence of her monumental 1961 work, she writes, "…(I am) content and happy to believe that ecstatic experiences are wholly human experiences; that what men have worshipped since ecstatic experiences were known to them was their own creative and generalizing capacity, that the god they sometimes believed they had perceived in these experiences was indeed the *logos*." (Ecstasy in Secular and Religious Experiences, p.374)

Take courage, for the human race is divine – Greek Philosopher, Sixth Century, BCE

D – THE LEVELS OF PEAK EXPERIENCES AND MYSTICAL STATES

David R. Hawkins, MD, Ph.D., in his provocative 2002 book, The Eye of the I, speaks of the relative scarcity of the condition known as mystical union with God: "To know God via direct experience is extremely rare. It occurs to less than one person in more than ten million people." (p. 149)

Clearly there are distinctions to be made in this matter. Not all PEs are created equal. We have used the term 'peak experience' – following Maslow and many others – in an almost generic way, as described in Chapter One. Although we do believe that man is wired for transcendence and is evolving to ever higher states, it is clear that not every PE automatically raises one to an exalted state of spiritual attainment. PEs, like the sun and rain, happen to everybody. While they may, and often do, move one towards a more open, serious, hopeful view of life, for the most part they do not bring instant enlightenment.

That people can prepare themselves for transcendent, mystical states is attested to by many centuries of men and women living in contemplative communities which, by their very nature, foster these states of consciousness. Ken Wilbur (See Chapter one) spoke of those states and stages of conscious evolution. Even in our own day, thousands of monks and nuns – of various religious persuasions – live well-organized lives of quiet diligence and devotion, spending many hours daily in meditation and contemplation, seeking to open their minds and hearts to transcendence.

They are usually not seeking peak experiences as such and for their own sake. Monastic teachers and trainers, in fact, often warn neophytes that such sensate experiences are potentially dangerous and should be avoided, lest they interfere with the goal of unity with the transcendent. Powerful PEs can be 'attractive hazards', luring the students (of whatever age) from their goal of total union with the divine, i.e., total enlightenment, to the more immediate purpose of producing PEs for the profound elation and joy that come with them. In fact, it is very common for meditative seekers to endure periods of mental and spiritual aridity. For example, modern day saint Mother Theresa of Calcutta, and medieval mystic, St. John of the Cross, both experienced long periods of profound mental and spiritual distress, a condition which St. John called "the dark night of the soul".

In this regard, many of the persons who submitted PEs for this book wrote of how their transcendent moments were so profound and beautiful that their hearts yearn for repeat performances. Once you have been to the mountain-top, it is difficult to return to the flat lands of the prairie.

This book is not written to be a guide for contemplative monks and nuns, practitioners of the spiritual path, or other devotees of the contemplative life. Rather, our more mundane purposes are to expand the knowledge of the general public, to remove artificial barriers to high moments of mountain-top experiences, and to encourage our striving for the farther reaches of the human spirit, for the betterment of us individually and for the evolution of the race.

E. RIGHT AND LEFT BRAIN: THE ONE AND THE MANY

When 37 year old brain scientist Jill Bolte Taylor, Ph.D., suffered a stroke on December 10, 1996, not only did her life radically change, but our knowledge of the human brain (and of peak experiences) changed as well. Ten years later, in 2006, she published the remarkable memoir about her life during and since that event, My Stroke of Insight: A Brain Scientist's Personal Journey.

Harvard educated, Dr. Taylor was named one of Time Magazine's 100 Most Influential People in the World in 2008. A neuroanatomist by profession, she was able to understand, though only dimly at times, what was happening to her on that fateful morning. "As the damaged left side of her brain – the rational , grounded, detail- and time- oriented side – swung in and out of function, Taylor alternated between two distinct and opposite realities: the euphoric nirvana of the intuitive and kinesthetic right brain, in which she felt a sense of complete well-being and peace, and the logical, sequential left brain, which recognized Jill was having a stroke and enabled her to seek help before she was lost completely". (from book jacket)

Those of us interested in peak experiences will immediately be alerted to words such as 'euphoric nirvana', 'intuitive', feelings of 'complete well-being and peace'. These are words often used by peakers to explain their mountain-top experiences. *Clearly PEs are primarily right hemispheric events during which the judgmental left hemisphere is mute and asleep.*

It took eight years for Jill Taylor to completely recover from her stroke and subsequent brain surgery. In spite of this most arduous journey back to normalcy (with the irreplaceable assistance of her devoted mother), Taylor now believes that the stroke was the best thing that could have happened to her because of the many profound lessons she learned about herself and about the nature of reality. She writes exquisite passages, using a deft combination of day and night language, describing these experiences.

...And here, deep within the absence of earthly temporality, the boundaries of my earthly body dissolved and I melted into the universe.

...Swathed in an unfolding sense of liberation and transformation, the essence of my consciousness shifted into a state that felt amazingly similar to my experience in Thetaville. I'm no authority, but I think the Buddhists would say I entered the mode of existence they call Nirvana.(p 49)

...I felt like a genie liberated from its bottle. The energy of my spirit seemed to flow like a great whale gliding through a sea of silent euphoria. Finer that the finest of pleasures we can experience as human beings, this absence of physical

boundary was one of glorious bliss. As my consciousness dwelled in a flow of sweet tranquility, it was obvious to me that I would never be able to squeeze the enormousness of my spirit back inside this tiny cellular matrix. (p 67)

While working mightily with her doctors and caretakers to return to normal functioning, i.e. regaining the use of the rational gifts of the left hemisphere and regaining healthy equilibrium between the two 'brains', Dr. Taylor is critical of the current scientific view which commonly denigrates the character of the right brain in order to extol the qualities of the left.

"Most commonly, the character of our right mind has been ridiculed and portrayed in an extremely unflattering light, simply because it does not understand verbal language or comprehend linear thought. In the case of the Dr. Jekyll and Mr. Hyde analogy, our right hemisphere personality is depicted as an uncontrollable, potentially violent, moronic, rather despicable ignoramus, which is not even conscious, and without whom we would probably be better off! In vast contrast, our left mind has routinely been touted as linguistic, sequential, methodical, rational, smart, and the seat of our consciousness". (p 132,133)

Having experienced at first hand the power, enormity and beauty of the isolated right brain, Taylor knows that she can never be the same as she was in the past.

We conclude our limited review of Dr. Taylor's stimulating and powerful book by quoting these two passages, one describing her joy, the other summarizing her Stroke of Insight, the latter addressing directly, it seems to me, "the higher reaches of human nature".

If I had to choose one word to describe the feeling I feel at the core of my right mind, I would have to say *joy*. My right

mind is thrilled to be alive. I experience a feeling of awe when I consider that I am simultaneously capable of being at *one* with the universe, while having an individual identity whereby I move into the world and manifest positive change...If you have lost your ability to experience joy, rest assured the circuitry is still there... -(p 171)

The two halves of my brain don't just perceive and think in different ways at a neurological level, but they demonstrate very different values based on the types of information they perceive, and thus exhibit very different personalities. *My stroke of insight is that at the core of my right hemisphere consciousness is a character that is directly connected to my feeling of deep inner peace. It is committed to the expression of peace, love, joy, and compassion in the world*. (p133)

(italics and underlining added)

The character Taylor refers to, the discovery and knowledge of which is her "stroke of insight" is, we suggest, the same reality that Huna calls the High Self.

It seems appropriate to end this discussion with the above insights of 'the brain scientist who had a stroke', Dr. Jill Bolte Taylor. The marvels of the human mind and brain continue to fascinate us. Each new discovery from the researchers adds to the sense of awe at the staggering potential of the human being. "The farther reaches of human nature" are, of course, based within or, at least, dependent upon, the eight pound glob of grey matter that resides in our heads. The experience and eloquence of Dr. Taylor educates our left hemisphere while it fascinates our right brain.

SUMMARY OF CHAPTER TEN   *We have briefly considered five areas, the combination of which might help us to explain and wrap our minds around what happens in a peak experience. The gestalt theory proposed by what is now known as Gestalt Psychology may help us grasp the* concept of knowledge that comes to us whole rather than a bit at a time. Second, the filter theory speaks of the safeguards Nature has set up for us humans lest we be overwhelmed by an onrush of reality. Third, the Huna philosophy provides, for some of us, a common language to help explain what transpires during a PE. Next, we made distinctions among the levels of mystical experience. Finally, we presented hopefully clarifying concepts from the stoke experience of the brain scientist, Dr. Jill Bolte Taylor, from her book, *Stroke of Insight*.

The final chapter will speak, however falteringly, of the unifying goal of all PEs - evolutionary development.

PEAK EXPERIENCES – FORWARD LEAPS FOR EVOLUTION

Evolution and peak experiences go hand-in-hand. As the lyrics of the old song "Love and Marriage" put it, you can't have one without the other. Individual lives affect the totality of humanity. It was always so; it is true today; it will always be true. It is natural law.

In a general sense, peak experiences, i.e., new insights into new possibilities, have been the motivating force for every major positive advance in human culture.

In this final chapter we will suggest that the obvious acceleration of the speed of modern change and very recent breakthroughs in our understanding of the spectacular capabilities of the human brain presage a profound and significant speed-up in the evolutionary process. Assuming we can update our ancient, non-functional understandings of God and man, and not kill one another with weapons of mass destruction in the name of a Higher Power, there is hope for the future, hope that we can not only survive, but prosper.

It seems to many that the speed of evolutionary change in our day is greatly increasing. Many leaders in various fields of human endeavor have noted that time itself seems to be going faster. Haven't you, the reader, noticed this? Now, time itself, the measure of change, cannot be speeding up, but the amount of change that we are experiencing and measuring, the sheer amount of new data coming at us, is surely increasing due to the accelerating pace of developmental change.

The book <u>Future Shock</u> was written in 1970 by the sociologist and futurist Alvin Toffler. It had a great and almost instant success and sold over six million copies. Two later Toffler books further developed his theme that the rate of change is actually toxic to us, that we are being overwhelmed by the enormous stresses caused by the rapid changes we are undergoing as we move from an industrial society to a "super-industrial society".

Toffler sounded the alarm – *and that was over 40 years ago!* Obviously the rate of change is continuing to accelerate and there is much evidence that the escalation is even increasing its speed, as he predicted it would.

Toffler concluded,

To survive, to avert what we have termed "future shock", the individual must become infinitely more adaptable and capable than before. He must search out totally new ways to anchor himself, for all the old roots – religion, nation, community, family or profession – are now shaking under the hurricane impact of the accumulated thrust.

It is the thesis of this book that Toffler is correct and that only an increase in the number, and perhaps the intensity, of peak experiences, mountain-

*top moments, altered-state events, can move humanity quickly enough from
a status quo inadequate to the survival needs of the present and future to
a higher state of consciousness that will give us the wherewithal to survive
and thrive as a species.*

INCREASING NUMBER OF PEAK EXPERIENCES

Jesuit paleontologist Teilhard de Chardin believed that mystical
experiences would become more common as man (evolution)
progressed. "I am more and more convinced - judging from my
own infinitesimal experience – that the process is indeed possible,
and is actually in operation, and that it will psychologically trans-
figure the world of tomorrow. (Quoted in Greeley, Ecstasy, p.31)

It is clear from recent statistical studies that the number of PEs
being reported has been increasing. Although reports differ from
one another regarding the percentages of people who report PEs
(depending partly on how the questions are asked), the trend is
definitely upwards. As early as 1974, researcher Andrew Greeley
reported that "In our research (based on interviews with almost
1500 people) there is evidence that one-half of the American population would report having experience of union with 'a powerful
spiritual force that draws me out of myself'. Almost one-fifth would
report frequent such experiences." (Greeley, Ecstasy, p 11)

More recent research confirms and updates the above. Besides
the startling increase in the number of NDEs (near-death experiences) cited in chapter one, we list below just six examples of
statements from researchers and scholars about the increase in
the number of persons   reporting PEs.

**"Nearly half of those surveyed, Pew (of Pew Forum) found,
have had a religious or mystical experience. (Magazine
"The Week" – Dec 25, 2009 - January 8, 2010, p. 21)**

Kevin Todeschi, CEO of the Association for Research and Enlightenment, author of <u>God In Real Life: Personal Encounters With the Divine</u> (2009) easily found over 100 individuals from all walks of life who wished to participate in his study of altered-state experiences.

For his inspiring 2005 book, <u>The Translucent Revolution: How People Just Like You Are Waking Up and Changing the World</u>, Arjuna Ardagh interviewed literally thousands of people: "dentists, hairdressers, housewives and hoboes...politicians, drug dealers and my tax consultant.... All over the world, from every imaginable background and belief, people report the trance of separation is being broken. *For the majority, this radical awakening has occurred within the past fifteen years.* (Italics added) *(*pp. 30,31*)*...At the time of this writing (published 2005) that means we are witnessing a shift in collective consciousness that is less than two decades old." (p. 61)

Award-winning journalist Barbara Bradley Hagerty estimated in her 2009 book, <u>Fingerprints of God: The Search for the Science of Spirituality</u>, that 60% of Americans "report that they have had an experience of the presence of God or a 'patterning' of events that persuades them that they are a part of a cosmic design." (p. 150)

Since 1969, the Alister Hardy Trust, established at Manchester College in England by a scientist, has collected accounts of over 6,000 religious experiences from people of all ages and backgrounds. It is interesting to note, in view of the science/spirituality focus propounded by this book, that Sir Alister Hardy (1896-1985) was a British marine biologist and Professor at Oxford who believed that the nonmaterial side of life was of extreme importance in providing science with a complete account of the evolutionary process.

Author Jack Canfield: "There is a curriculum raining down on the planet. Anyone who is half awake is picking up on it. More people are aware and are awakening to these energies. More and more people have a sense that life has a higher purpose, a sense of connecting to something more deeply spiritual, something beyond the theological concepts they've been taught in church".

Jack Canfield (Quoted in Ardagh's <u>Transcendent Revolution</u> (p. 265)

Why this change? Why are there many more "outbreaks of spirit" in the last few decades? Many thoughtful observers believe that it is the highest elements in human nature responding to our imperative need to wake up, in order that we may solve the grievous problems affecting our world and threatening our continued existence.

In response to unprecedented perils threatening our welfare, and perhaps our very existence, something deep inside human nature seems to be awakening in our time. Carl Jung (1875-1961) called it "this momentous transformation" which is absolutely necessary for our survival.

A mood of universal destruction and renewal has set its mark on our age. This mood makes itself felt everywhere, politically, socially, and philosophically. We are living in what the Greeks called the kairos – the right moment – for a "metamorphosis of the gods", of the fundamental principles and symbols. This peculiarity of our time, which is certainly not of our conscious choosing, is the expression of the unconscious man within us who is changing. *Coming generations will have to take account of this momentous transformation if humanity is not to destroy itself through the might of its own technology and science.* So much is at stake and so much depends on the psychological constitution of modern humans.

(The Undiscovered Self, p. 304) (Italics added.)

The following are further quotes from Jung on the importance of changing and upgrading, first the individual, then human society as a whole.

A change in the attitude of the individual can bring about a renewal in the spirit of the nations. ("Essay on Contemporary Events")

The whole future, the whole history of the world, ultimately springs as a gigantic summation from these hidden sources in individuals. In our most private and subjective lives we are not only the passive witnesses of our age, and its sufferers, but also its makers. We make our epoch.
(The Meaning of Psychology for Modern Man, p. 149)

A NEW KIND OF HUMAN?

Some people, including some savants and forward looking scholars, believe that evolution has been and is even now at work producing a new kind of human, that the human race is developing new capacities because something different, something added to our characteristics, is absolutely necessary if the race is to survive.

An impressive array of thoughtful observers can be presented to attest to these substantial developments. Abraham Maslow himself was intrigued by the notion of "future time". He believed that in the core of our being lay the seeds of our further becoming. "No theory of psychology", he wrote, "will ever be complete that does not centrally incorporate the concept that man has his future within him, dynamically active at the present moment". (Hoffman, The Right to Be Human, p.154)

Maslow was amazed as he considered the implications of his study of the self-actualized population samples. In a never published introduction for what was to be his 'magnum opus', he wrote in 1944:

...man has infinite potentiality, which, properly used, could make his life like his fantasies of heaven. In potentiality, he is the most awe-inspiring phenomenon in the universe, the most creative, the most ingenious. Throughout the ages, philosophers have sought to understand the true, the beautiful, and to speak for its forces. Now we know that the best place to look for them is in man himself.

(Hoffman, <u>The Right to Be Human</u>, p. 165)

OUR PLASTIC, MALLEABLE BRAINS

Neuroscience has recently had a breakthrough discovery with enormous implications for peak experiences and for evolution: the human brain has the ability to grow and change throughout our lifetimes in ways we did not previously realize. The name given this concept is neuroplasticity.

Startling discoveries about how the brain can change are described in the 2007 book, <u>The Brain That Changes Itself; Stories of Personal Triumph from the</u> <u>Frontiers of Brain Science</u>, by Norman Doidge, a psychiatrist and researcher on the faculties of both Columbia University and the University of Toronto. The author points out that, until now, mainstream medicine and science believed that brain anatomy was fixed and unalterable. This was quite a destructive belief, leading to a kind of "neurological nihilism".

...The theory of the unchanging brain decreed that people who were born with brain or mental limitations, or who sustained brain damage, would be limited or damaged for life. Scientists who wondered if the healthy brain might be improved or preserved through activity or mental exercise were told not to waste their time. A neurological nihilism – a sense that treatment for many brain problems was ineffective or even unwarranted – had taken hold, and it spread through our culture, *even stunting our overall view of human nature. Since the brain could not change, human*

nature, which emerges from it, seemed necessarily fixed
and unalterable as well.
- Preface, p. xviii (Italics added)

But now, says Dr. Doidge, we know that the brain can change its own structure and function through thought and activity. "Like all revolutions, this one will have profound effects" in many different fields of human endeavor, including the humanities, the social and physical sciences, and all forms of training.

The plasticity of the brain - its ability to grow and meet new and as yet unprecedented demands - is crucial to our understandings of peak experiences and their role in evolutionary progress. Even before neuroplasticity became the new buzzword in scientific circles, it was obvious that the brain could adapt in rather startling ways to the demands of cultural necessity, leading to the old adage that 'Necessity is the mother of invention'.

Researcher Doidge points out, quoting from one of the leading 'neuroplasticians', Michael Merzenich, that we all have culturally modified brains, "vastly different, in fine detail, from the brains of our ancestors" (p. 288). At each major stage of our development, humankind had the capacity to learn complex new skills and these were passed down to subsequent generations, not via genetic change, but through cultural necessity or expectations. (I see a homely example of this in my children who are much more adept at using computers than I, and my grandchildren who exhibit what seems to me unusual and apparently untaught dexterity and skill in various technological communication instruments far beyond my capacity to understand, much less use.)

Doidge cites the amazing example of 'Sea Gypsies', nomadic people who live in a cluster of tropical islands in the Burmese archipelago and off the west coast of Thailand.

A wandering water tribe, they learn to swim before they learn to walk, and live over half their lives in boats on the open sea, where they are often born and die. They survive

by harvesting clams and sea cucumbers. Their children dive down, often thirty feet beneath the water's surface, and pluck up their food, including small morsels of marine life, and have done so for centuries. By learning to lower their heart rate, they can stay under water twice as long as most swimmers. They do this without any diving equipment. One tribe, the Sulu, dive over seventy-five feet for pearls.

But what distinguishes these children, for our purposes, is that they can see clearly at these great depths, without goggles. Most human beings cannot see clearly under water because as sunlight passes through water, it is bent or 'refracted', so that light doesn't land where it should on the retina. (pp. 288, 289)

Doidge states that the Sea Gypsies have learned to control the size of their lenses, constricting them 22 percent. That this is not the product of a unique genetic endowment is proved by the fact that another researcher has taught Swedish children to constrict their pupils so they, too, could see under water. (p. 289)

It is clear that the brain can change and adapt to meet new conditions. The fact that we humans are still here on planet earth attests to the malleability, the plasticity of the brain.

Our looming planetary crises are calling for a series of profound changes which, *in the normal course of events,* will be preceded and announced by profound peak experiences happening with increased frequency. That such experiences do not seem normal to us is because we have grown accustomed to perceiving PEs as extraordinary events, rather than the natural progression of a process of evolution, a process so slow that we are not able to see it occurring. We have not appreciated the immensity and grandeur of what Maslow termed "the farther reaches of human nature," nor, perhaps, the immensity and grandeur of the evolutionary process itself.

This concept is well expressed by author Kathy L.Callahan in her 2005 book, <u>The Multisensory Human : The Evolution of the Soul.</u>

> **The transformation that the human species is about to face may seem 'instantaneous' because we are seeing only the end result and not the entire process. That is why some people have leaped to the conclusion that these changes are instantaneous developments, miraculous acts of God, or the result of alien intervention. We need to understand that they are the natural result of biological changes occurring within the internal structure and function of the human brain, the next step upward on the evolutionary spiral our species has been traveling for millions of years. (p. 85)**

NEEDED: ONGOING REDEFINITIONS OF DEITY AND MANKIND

As evolution constantly expands our knowledge of the universe, our planet and ourselves, *it is apparent that we need constant revisions of our concept of Deity.* As has been pointed out by many scholars, philosophers and theologians, part of our problem is the very vocabulary we use. Friedrich Nietzsche's proclamation that 'God Is Dead' more than a century ago can be understood by all – believers, atheists and agnostics – to apply at least to the use of the word 'God' which generates such diverse, often contradictory, responses.

For the remainder of this book (unless quoting others) I will use the word Deity when referring to the concept and reality of what we used to call 'God'. This small step is a feeble attempt to indicate that, for almost all mankind, the denotation and connotation of the old word 'God' are :

a) much too narrow;

b) totally personal and subjective;

c) clearly inadequate to express the totally incomprehensible Deity;

d) garbled by historical uses and abuses of the word;

e) likely to cause confusion because readers will perceive the meaning of the word very differently from one another due to their own personal educations, cultures, and histories. For example, Islamic fundamentalists and Christian fundamentalists may have surprisingly different definitions of 'God'. If certain words no longer designate common meanings, it seems counterproductive to use them.

It appears to this author that persons who seriously study the phenomena of peak experiences, transcendental or mystical states, etc. will soon discover that they need to widen considerably their own concepts, not only of Deity, but also their concepts of what human nature is and what it is, perhaps, becoming. The example of Abraham Maslow is instructive here. He became more and more convinced that human nature itself was increasingly profound and 'Deitylike', although he did not believe in Deity.

In 1961, when we knew less about the universe than we do now, Minister John B. Phillips wrote a small book titled <u>Your God Is Too Small</u>. That could well be the theme song of human history with its anthropomorphic gods, narrow sectarian world views, and restrictive religious concepts which have caused such hatred, confusion, mayhem, and havoc – all in the name of a loving Deity.

Examples follow of philosophers, authors and scholars who learned to enlarge their original views about the Deity and its relationship with Man.

Robert Wright: At the end of his <u>Nonzero: The Logic of Human Destiny</u>, he speculates, "Maybe history, is, as various thinkers have suggested, not so much the product of divinity as the realization of divinity - assuming our species is up to the challenge, that is". (p. 332)

Joseph Chilton Pierce: "A major argument of this book has been that transcendence, the ability to rise and go beyond limitation and restraint, is our biological birthright, built into us genetically and blocked by enculturation". - <u>The Biology of Transcendence: A Blueprint of the Human Spirit</u>, (p. 225)

Carl Jung: "I cannot define for you what God is. I can only say that my work has proved empirically that the pattern of God exists in every man and that this pattern has at its disposal the greatest of all his energies for transformation and transfiguration of his natural being. Not only the meaning of man's life, but his renewal and his institutions depend on this conscious relationship with this pattern of his collective unconscious." - From a letter to his friend, Laurens van der Post. (Quoted in <u>Carl Jung- Wounded Healer of the Soul</u> by Claire Dunne, p. 202)

Barbara Bradley Hagerty: "...What I did not expect in my search (for the science of spirituality) was a radical re-definition of God," wrote Hagerty near the end of her masterful 2009 study. Yet, this was necessary for the author herself.

– <u>Fingerprints of God: The Search for the Science of Spirituality</u>, p. 277

TOMORROW'S GOD

1. Tomorrow's God does not require anyone to believe in God.
2. Tomorrow's God is without gender, size, shape, color, or any of the characteristics of an individual living being.
3. Tomorrow's God talks with everyone, all the time.
4. Tomorrow's God is separate from nothing, but is everywhere Present, the All In All, the Alpha and the Omega, the Beginning and the End, the Sum Total of Everything that ever was, is now, and ever shall be.
5. Tomorrow's God is not a singular Super Being, but the extraordinary process called Life.
6. Tomorrow's God is ever changing.
7. Tomorrow's God is needless.
8. Tomorrow's God does not ask to be served, but is the Servant of all of Life.
9. Tomorrow's God will be unconditionally loving, nonjudgmental, noncondemning, and nonpunishing.

                                        - Neale Donald Walsch,
            - Tomorrow's God: Our Greatest Spiritual Challenge

---

Cell scientist Bruce Lipton, our case study of the last chapter, had this interesting comment about the definition of Deity. He has a skeptical reader ask: The Deity is here? He *knows* the Deity? Lipton responds, "...Yes, yes, I believe I do. I must admit that I don't know all the Deity personally, for I don't know all of you. For God's sake, there are over six billion of YOU! And, to be more fully honest, I don't really know all the members of the plant and animal kingdom either, though I believe they also comprise God."

                                        - The Biology of Belief, p. 28)

FINAL ENCOURAGING WORDS FROM THOMAS BERRY

It is fitting that Thomas Berry, cultural historian and eco-theologian (to whose memory this book is dedicated) is given the last word. Much of his life was devoted to the task of awakening his fellow humans to their role in saving the planet from the mindless destruction that our collective ignorance was causing. Yet, he realized that, dire as the situation was, hope was needed. The following quotation is taken from the concluding paragraph of one of his profound books, <u>The Great Work</u>.

In the immense story of the universe, (the fact that) so many dangerous moments have been navigated successfully is some indication that the universe is for us rather than against us. We need only summon these forces to our support in order to succeed. Although the human challenge to these purposes must never be underestimated, it is difficult to believe that the larger purposes of the universe or of the planet Earth will ultimately be thwarted. (p. 201)

SUMMARY OF CHAPTER ELEVEN

The prime thesis of this book is reiterated – that peak experiences that happen to individuals are, in fact, the main vehicles for the evolution and progress of the human species. The increasing number of PEs at the current time may presage a coming evolutionary leap of significant proportions. Recent research indicates our brains are far more plastic and malleable than we realized before. It is important that mankind adjust to our ever increasing power and stature by constantly updating our ideas both of Deity and of the ever expanding 'farther reaches of human nature'.

AFTERWORD

Among the lessons I have learned from writing this book, lessons that I am grateful for and marvel at, three of the most significant are:

1. Peak experiences essentially have to do with knowing.
2. Most PEs come with almost lightning speed.
3. Even the most profoundly significant PEs involve only a tiny shift in consciousness.

Lesson One – How People Learn

PEs essentially have to do with knowing; they are the gates whereby knowledge comes to humans. They are the pathways through which new and profound, life changing information and knowledge forces its way into human consciousness. Aristotelian philosophy teaches that all knowledge comes via the senses and certainly much of this world's does. But the knowledge that 'really counts', the knowledge that creates and changes worlds, does not come from this plane, at least not in the way we generally understand this physical level.

This view is essentially a Platonic way of looking at the world. How little we understand about this! We are like children in Toyland, full of awe and wonder. Perhaps this is perfectly fine and appropriate, at least at this stage of our evolution. Maybe we are like the 16th century shepherd of the frontispiece who is looking in amazement at other worlds that he is as yet incapable of understanding.

Lesson two – Instant Knowing

All peak experiences come suddenly, usually without any warning. Like a mental lightening bolt, they suddenly overwhelm our consciousness. They jolt us aware. The change is effected instantaneously. "In the twinkling of an eye" (to use a phrase from Paul's Letter to the Corinthians-I) they disarm the Robot that we use so well to shield us from over-amounts of reality.

A final example well illustrates these two aspects of most PEs. This comes from a dentist, James Reed, who looks back to a split second of time in 1970 when a profoundly meaningful conviction was given to him.

I was about nine months out of dental school and was living with my folks and treating the overflow patients of my family dentist in our small Northern Indiana town.

I was definitely unsettled as far as my chosen profession was concerned. My young mind had become that squirrel cage of unending thought as I wondered where I was headed in the world of Dentistry. Private practice didn't feel right, but what did feel right? That "figuring- it-all-out" squirrel cage of mind busyness ran on and on for days and weeks.

One late winter afternoon, returning to my dental operatory world from lunch, I stepped off the curb to cross the street, and *before my foot touched the pavement* a feeling had suddenly owned my being. It felt like a tuning fork – BOINNGG – had been struck in my sternum. *I was suddenly clear. I knew! It was right*. I would go back to Grad School in the Dental Specialty of Public Health.

Now, 34 years later, having found awesome fulfillment with Public Health, my personal niche in my profession, I have been certain to tell my three children that the answer to one of the biggest questions in my life came when "figuring it out" had given way to this Peak Experience from within.

---

3. A Tiny Shift of Consciousness

What has become clear to me, after considering hundreds of mountain-top experiences of people from the most varied backgrounds, is that *it takes only a very small change in perspective, only a slight tweaking of our conscious and unconscious attention, to become aware of very different realities and to allow peak experiences to come.*

There is apparently only a fine line, what William James called "the flimsiest of screens," separating what we consider our normal, waking consciousness from entirely different forms of consciousness. Well over one hundred years ago, American Psychologist William James (1842-1910), wrote a great deal about what we now call peak experiences. He wrote, "We may go through life without suspecting their existence, but apply the requisite stimulus, and at a touch they are there in all their completeness".

Assuming this is true, and assuming that having PEs is perceived as desirable – for oneself and one's world – can we also assume that the reason we don't have more PEs is because we hold too tightly to the mind-set, the relatively narrow world view that we, our families, our culture, have fashioned for us? This appears to be true.

Perhaps our next step will be to devise ways and means for us to release our unenlightened, robotic devotion to our individual narrow ways of perceiving the world so that we can allow for the possibility of other, richer ways which could arise from "the farther reaches of human nature."

THANKSGIVING

It has been a great joy to write this book. Hundreds of people have invited me into their innermost hearts to share their stories of up-liftment, joy and, often, ecstasy. Being privy to the best moments of people's lives is both humbling and exalting. Just as words can only falteringly express these transcendent moments, so it is with expressing the gratitude I feel to those who were willing to share with me – and with you readers – such personal epiphanies. We are profoundly grateful.

Gratitude also goes to the hundreds who assisted in the birth of this book. To Abraham Maslow, to the authors of the extensive bibliography – you are all my heroes, heroines and benefactors. To those who helped in so many ways – to former students and past and present friends, to editors and readers, to cheerleaders and critics – many thanks. A warm tribute goes to Philip Thurman for helpful advice on how to enter the publishing world.

An array of gratitude goes to Romella Hart-O'Keefe – generous spouse and helpmate, loving companion, and fellow-seeker after joy, beauty and happiness. It was she who mid-wifed this book into being. She even provided the title.

BIBLIOGRAPHY

Andrews, Julie. <u>Home: A Memoir of My Early Years.</u> New York, NY. Hyperion: 2008.

Ardagh, Arjuna. <u>The Translucent Revolution: How People Just Like You are Waking Up and Changing the World.</u> Novato, CA: New World Library, 2005.

Arkin, Alan. <u>Halfway Through the Door: An Actor's Journey Toward the Self.</u> New York, NY: Harper and Row,1979.

Armstrong, Karen. <u>The Case for God</u>. New York, NY: Alfred A. Knopf, 2009.

_____. <u>A History of God: The 4,000 Year Quest of Judaism, Christianity and Islam</u>. New York, NY: Ballantine Books, 1993.

Assagioli, Roberto, M.D. <u>The Act of Will.</u> New York, NY: Penguin Books, 1973.

Atwater, P.M.H. with David H. Morgan. <u>The Complete Idiot's Guide to Near-Death Experiences.</u> Indianapolis, IN: Alpha Books/Macmillan, 2000.

Bays, Brandon. <u>The Journey: A Practical Guide To Healing Your Life and Setting Yourself Free</u>. New York, NY: Fireside/Simon and Schuster, 1999.

Berney, Charlotte. <u>Fundamentals of Hawaiian Mysticism.</u> Freedom, CA: Crossing Press, 2000, 2001.

Berry, Thomas. <u>Evening Thoughts: Reflecting on Earth as Sacred Community.</u> San Francisco, CA: Sierra Book Clubs, 2006.

_____. The Great Work: Our Way Into the Future. New York, NY: Three Rivers Press, 1999.

_____. The Sacred Universe: Earth, Spirituality in the Twenty-First Century. New York, NY: Columbia University Press, 2009.

Bonny, Helen L.& Louis M. Savary. Music and Your Mind: Listening With a New Consciousness. Barrytown, NY: Station Hill Press, 1973, 1990.

Borg, Marcus J. Meeting Jesus Again For the First Time: The Historical Jesus and the Heart of Contemporary Faith. New York, NY: Harper Collins, 1994.

Boroson, Martin. One-Moment Meditation: Stillness for People on the Go. Winter Road Publishing, 2009.

Caddy, Peter with Jeremy Slocombe and Renath Caddy. In Perfect Timing: Memoirs of a Man for the New Millenium. Forres, Scotland: Findhorn Press, 1996.

Calhoun, Peter. Soul on Fire: A transformational Journey From Priest to Shaman. Carlsbad, CA: Hay House, 2007.

Callahan, Kathy L. Multisensory Human: The Evolution of the Soul. Virginia Beach, VA: A.R.E. Press, 1996, 2005.

Caponigro, Andy. The Miracle of the Breath: Mastering Fear, Healing Illness, and Experiencing the Divine. Novato, CA: New World Library, 2005.

Cass, Hyla, M.D. and Patrick Holford. Natural Highs: Supplements, Nutrition, and Mind-Body Techniques To Help You Feel Good All the Time. New York, NY: Avery/Penguin Putnam, Inc., 2002.

Church, Dawson, Ph.D. The Genie in Your Genes: Epigenetic Medicine and the New Biology of Intention. Santa Rosa, CA: Elite Books, 2007.

Cohen, Andrew. Living Enlightenment: A Call for Evolution Beyond Ego. Lenox, MA: Moksha Press, 2002.

Collins, Billy. Sailing Around the Room, New York, NY: Random House, 2001.

Coxhead, Nora. The Relevance of Bliss: A Contemporary Exploration of Mystic Experience. New York, NY: St. Martin's Press, 1985.

Dear, John. Transfiguration: A Meditation on Transforming Ourselves and Our World. New York, NY: Image/Doubleday, 2007.

Deikman, Arthur J., M.D. Deautomatization and the Mystic Experience. From website: Dr. Arthur Deikman.

DeRopp, Robert S. The Master Game: Pathways to Higher Consciousness Beyond the Drug Experience. New York, NY.: Delacorte Press, 1968.

Doidge, Norman, M.D. The Brain That Changes Itself: Stories of Personal Triumph From the Frontiers of Brain Science. New York, NY: Penguin, 2007.

Dourley, John P. The Illness That We Are: A Jungian Critique of Christianity. Toronto, Canada: Inner City Books, 1984.

Dowd, Michael. Thank God for Evolution: How the Marriage of Science and Religion Will Transform Your Life and Our World. New York, NY: Penguin Group, 2007.

Dunne, Claire. Carl Jung: Wounded Healer of the Soul: An Illustrated Biography. New York, NY: Parabola Books, 2000.

Dyer, Wayne W. The Power of Intention: Learning to Co-Create Your World Your Way. Carlsbad, CA: Hay House, 2004.

Ehrenreich, Barbara. Dancing in the Streets: A History of Collective Joy. New York, NY: Metropolitan Books/ Henry Holt, 2007.

el Sadat, Anwar. In Search of Identity: An Autobiography. New York, NY: Harper & Row, 1977.

Ferrucci, Piero. <u>Inevitable Grace: Breakthroughs in the Lives of Great Men and Women:Guide to Your Self-Realization.</u> Los Angeles, CA: Jeremy P. Tarcher, Inc., 1990.

_____. <u>The Power of Kindness: The Unexpected Benefits of Leading a Compassionate Life.</u> New York, NY: Jeremy P. Tarcher/ Penguin, 2006.

Fillmore, Myrtle. <u>Myrtle Fillmore's Healing Letters</u>. Unity Village, MO: Unity Books, 1986.

Fox, Matthew. <u>The Hidden Spirituality of Men: Ten Metaphors to Awaken the Sacred Masculine.</u> Novato, CA: New World Library, 2008.

_____. <u>Original Blessing.</u> New York, NY: Tarcher/ Putnam, 1983,2000.

_____. <u>Whee! We, wee All the Way Home…A Guide to a Sensual, Prophetic Spirituality.</u> Santa Fe, NM: Bear & Company, 1981.

Frazier, Jan. <u>When Fear Falls Away:</u> The Story of a Sudden Awakening. San Francisco, CA: Weiser Books, 2007.

Gallup, George, Jr. <u>Adventures in Immortality.</u> New York, NY: McGraw-Hill, 1982.

Gilbert, Elizabeth. <u>Eat, Pray, Love: One Woman's Search for Everything Across Italy, India and Indonesia.</u> Penguin Books, 2007.

Gladwell, Malcolm. <u>The Tipping Point: How Little Things Can Make a Big Difference.</u> New York, NY: Back Bay Books; Little, Brown & Co., 200, 2002.

Greeley, Andrew M. <u>Ecstasy: A Way of Knowing.</u> Englewood Cliffs, NJ: Prentice-Hall, 1974.

Green, Elmer, Ph.D. <u>The Ozawkie Book of the Dead: Alzheimer's Isn't What you Think It Is.</u> Los Angeles, CA: Philosophical Research Society, 2001.

Grof, Stanislav, M.D., Ph.D. <u>When the Impossible Happens: Adventures In Non-Ordinary Realities.</u> Boulder, CO: Sounds True, Inc., 2006.

Hadley, Jennifer. "Man On a Mission". <u>Science of Mind</u>, December, 2008.

Haggerty, Barbara Bradley. <u>Fingerprints of God: The Search for the Science of Spirituality.</u> New York, NY: Riverbend Books (Penguin Books), 2009.

Haidt, Jonathon. <u>The Happiness Hypothesis: Finding Modern Truth in Ancient Wisdom.</u> Perseus Books, 2006.

Happold, F.C. <u>Mysticism: A Study and an Anthology.</u> Middlesex, England: Penguin Books, Ltd., 1964.

Hawkins, David R., M.D., Ph.D. <u>The Eye of the I: From Which Nothing Is Hidden</u>. Sedona, AZ: Veritas, 2001.

_____. <u>Power VS Force-The Hidden Determinants of Human Behavior.</u> Carlsbad, CA: Hay House, 1995, 2002.

Hoffman, Edward. <u>The Right To Be Human: A Biography of Abraham Maslow.</u> Los Angeles, CA: Jeremy P. Tarcher, 1988.

_____. <u>Visions of Innocence: Spiritual and Inspirational Experiences of Childhood.</u> Boston, MA and London, England: Shambala, 1992.

Hoffman, Enid. <u>Huna: A Beginner's Guide.</u> Atglen, PA: Whitford Press, 1976, 1981.

Huttner, Hilary. <u>Mystical Delights.</u> Incline Village, NV: Frontline Systems, 1996.

Jaxon-Bear, Eli. <u>Sudden Awakening Into Direct Realization</u>. Tiburn, CA: H.J. Kramer/ New World Library, 2004.

Johnson, Robert A. <u>Ecstasy: Understanding the Psychology of Joy.</u> New York, NY: Harper & Row, 1989.

Johnson, Raynor C. The Imprisoned Splendor: An Approach to Reality. Wheaton, IL: Theosophical Publishing House, 1953.

_____. Watcher on the Hill. Edinburgh, Scotland: Hodder and Stroughton, Ltd., 1959.

Joseph, Frank, (Editor). Sacred Sites: A guidebook to Sacred Centers and Mysterious Places in the United States. St. Paul, MN: Llewellyn Publications, 1992.

Jung, Carl. The Undiscovered Self: The Problem of the Individual in Modern Society. New York, NY: Random House, 1970.

King, Martin Luther, Dr. Stride Toward Freedom. New York, NY: Harper and Row, 1958.

Koerner, Brendan I. "Secret of AA: After 75 Years, We Don't Know How It Works." Wired Magazine, June 23, 2010.

Kuby, Lolette, Ph.D. Faith and the Placebo Effect: An Argument for Self-Healing. San Raphael, CA: Origin Press, 2004.

Laski, Marghanita. Ecstasy In Secular and Religious Experience. Los Angeles, CA: Jeremy P. Tarcher, Inc., 1961.

Le Shan, Lawrence, Ph.D. The Medium, The Mystic, and the Physicist: Toward a Central Theory of the Paranormal. New York, NY: Penguin, 1966, 1974.

Levoy, Gregg. Callings: Finding and Following an Authentic Life. New York, NY: Three Rivers Press/ Random House, 1997.

Lewis, C.S. Surprised By Joy. San Diego, CA: Harcourt Brace Janovich, 1956.

Lipton, Bruce H. The Biology of Belief: Understanding the Power of Consciousness, Matter and Miracles. Santa Rosa, CA: Elite Books, 2005.

Lonegren, Sig. Spiritual Dowsing: Tools For Exploring the Intangible Realms. Glastonbury, England: Gothic Image Publications, 1986, 2007.

Long, Max Freedom. The Secret Science At Work: The Huna Method As a Way of Life. Marina del Ray, CA: De Vorss, 1953.

McArthur, David and Bruce. The Intelligent Heart: Transform Your Life with the Laws of Love. Virginia Beach, VA: ARE Press, 1997.

McTaggart, Lynne. The Intention Experiment: Using Your Thoughts to Change Your Life and the World. New York, NY: Free Press/ Simon and Schuster, 2007.

Merton, Thomas. The Asian Journal. New York, NY: New Directions, 1973

Mitchell, Edgar D. Psychic Exploration: A Challenge for Science. New York, NY: G.P. Putnam's Sons, 1974.

_____. The Way of the Explorer: An Apollo Astronaut's Journey Through the Material and Mystical Worlds. Franklin Lakes, NJ: Career Press, 2008.

Monroe, Robert A. Journeys Out of the Body. Garden City, NY: Anchor Press/Doubleday, 1971,1973.

Moody, Raymond, (Editor). Life After Life. 1975.

Morehouse, David, Ph.D. Remote Viewing: The Complete User's Manual for Coordinate Remote Viewing. Boulder, CO: Sounds True, 2008.

Newberg, Andrew, M.D., Eugene D'Aquili, M.D. and Vince Rause. Why God Won't Go Away: Brain Science and the Biology of Belief. New York, NY: Ballentine Books, 2001, 2002.

Newfeld, Carly. Findhorn Book of Guidance and Intuition. Forres,Scotland: Findhorn Press,   2003.

Pagels, Elaine. Adam, Eve, and the Serpent. New York, NY: Vintage Books/ Random House, 1988.

Peace Pilgrim. Peace Pilgrim: Her Life and Work in Her Own Words. Ocean Tree Books, 1983.

Pearsall, Paul, Ph.D. The Beethoven Factor: <u>The New Positive Psychology of Hardiness, Happiness, Healing and Hope.</u> Charlottsville, VA: Hampton Roads, 2003.

_____. <u>Super Joy: In Love With Living.</u> New York, NY: Doubleday, 1988.

_____. <u>Wishing Wells: Making Your Every Wish Come True.</u> New York, NY: Hyperion, 2000.

Pennington, Judith. "The Meditation Experience." <u>Venture Inward</u>. Virginia Beach, VA:ARE_ January/ February, 2009.

Phillips, J.B. <u>Your God Is Too Small.</u> Second Edition, Scribner Book Company, 1964, 1987.

Richards, M.C. <u>Centering- In Pottery, Poetry, and the Person.</u> Middletown, CN: Wesleyan Press, 1962, 1989.

Russell, Peter. <u>Waking Up In Time: Finding Inner Peace in Times of Accelerating Change</u>. Novato, CA: Origin Press, 1992, 1998.

Russell, William F. with Taylor Brench. <u>Second Wind: The Memories of an Opinionated Man.</u> Ballantine Books, 1979.

Sachs, Oliver. <u>Musicophilia: Tales of Music and the Brain.</u> New York, NY: Vintage/Random House, 2007,2008.

Sadat, Anwar. See el-Sadat.

Seligmon, Martin, E.P., Ph. D. <u>Authentic Happiness: Using the New Positive Psychology to Realize Your Potential for Lasting Fulfillment</u>. New York, NY: Free Press/Simon and Schuster, 2002.

Serrano, Sergio E. Ph.D. <u>The Three Spirits: Applications of Huna to Health, Prosperity, and Personal Growth.</u> Ambler, PA: Spiral Press, 2008.

Stahl, Louann. <u>A Most Surprising Song: Exploring the Mystical Experience.</u> Unity Village, MO: Unity Books, 1992.

Starke, Walter. "Circle Letter". Guadalupe Press. Winter 2009.

Starr, Irina. From These Waters: The Continuing Renewal. Ojai, CA: The Pilgrims Path, 1977, 1991.

_____. The Sound of Light: Experiencing the Transcendental. New York, NY: Philosophical Library, 1969.

Storr, Anthony. Music and the Mind. New York, NY: Ballantine Books/Random House, 1992.

Styron, William. Darkness Visible. New York, NY: Random House, 1990.

Tagore, Rathindranath. A Tagore Reader. Edited by Amiya Chakravarty. Boston, MA: Macmillan, 1961.

Tammet, Daniel. Embracing th Wide Sky: A Tour Across the Horizons of the Mind. New York, NY: Free Press (Simon & Schuster), 2009.

Tart, Charles T., Ph.D. The End of Materialism: How Evidence of the Paranormal Is Bringing Science and Spirit Together. Oakland, CA: New Harbinger & Noetic Books, 2009.

Taylor, Jill Bolte. My Stroke of Insight: A Brain Scientist's Personal Journey. New York, NY: Viking, 2006.

Todeschi, Kevin J. God in Real Life: Personal Encounters With the Divine. Virginia Beach, VA: 4th Dimension Press, 2009.

Tolle, Eckhart. The Power of Now: A Guide to Spiritual Enlightment. Novato, CA: New World Library, 1999, 2004.

Ullman, Robert and Judith Reichenberg-Ullman. Mystics, Masters, Saints and Sages: Stories of Enlightenment. Berkelet, CA: Conari Press, 2001.

Vahle, Neal. Torch-Bearer to Light the Way: The Life of Myrtle Fillmore. Mill Valley, CA: Open View Press, 1996.

Walker, Evan Harris. The Physics of Consciousness: The Quantum Mind and the Meaning of Life. New York, NY: Perseus Publishers, 2000.

Walsch, Neale Donald. <u>Tomorrow's God: Our Greatest Spiritual Challenge.</u> New York, NY: Atria/ Simon & Schuster, 2004.

Weiner, Eric. <u>The Geography of Bliss: One Grump's Search for the Happiest Places in the World.</u> New York, NY: Hachette Book Group, 2008.

White, John. (Editor) <u>The Highest State of Consciousness.</u> Garden City, NY: Doubleday, Anchor Books, 1972.

Wilson, Colin. <u>Dreaming to Some Purpose.</u> London, England: Arrow Books, 2004, 2005.

_____. <u>The Outsider.</u> New York, NY: Dell, 1956

_____. <u>Mysteries: An Investigation Into the Occult, the Paranormal and the Supernatural.</u> 2006.

_____. <u>New Pathways in Psychology: Maslow and the Post Freudian Revolution.</u> Taplinger Publishing Company, 1972-2008.

_____. <u>Poetry and Mysticism.</u> San Francisco, CA: City Lights Books, 1969.

_____. <u>Super Consciousness: The Quest for the Peak Experience.</u> London, England: Watkins Publishers, 2009.

Wise, Anna. <u>Awakening the Mind: A guide to Mastering the Power of Your Brain Waves.</u> New York, NY: Tarcher/Putnam, 2002.

_____. <u>The High Performance Mind.</u> New York, NY: Tarcher/ Putnam, 1995,1997.

COPYRIGHT/PERMISSIONS PAGE

ABOUT THE AUTHOR

Dr. Edward O'Keefe is a former Dean of Academic Affairs at a New York State community college. Before retiring from academic life, he taught English and Writing for 25 years and often assigned his students the writing of essays or poems about their peak experiences, 'mountaintop moments' of joy and inspiration. From this beginning, he developed a lifelong passion for the subject of peak experiences (PEs).

A native of Niagara Falls, NY, Dr. O'Keefe is a Myofascial Trigger Point Therapist. He lives with his wife, Romella, near Asheville, North Carolina. Their blended family consists of nine children, eleven grandchildren, one great-grandson and one cat. Ed and Romella maintain a lovely garden and teach various subjects, including EFT, Emotional Freedom Techniques. They are ordained non-denominational ministers and enjoy performing weddings together. They are also available to give workshops on Peak Experiences.

If you would like to share a peak experience or communicate with the author, visit www.peakexperience.info or email edrookeefe@att.net.

TOUCHING

Maybe, just maybe
There is a dimension of thought and feeling
Lying just behind the outstretched fingers of our mind –
A dimension we haven't really touched as yet.

Perhaps if we would extend ourselves –
Reach out beyond our thinking – we might touch it.
And, in touching,
Experience something new –
Yet – something known.

In so doing, we might soar... and sail...
And see... and feel...
And become

What we know we already are.

-Anonymous

Made in the USA
Lexington, KY
19 May 2013